THE *Second* POLITICALLY CORRECT SCRAPBOOK

By John and Laura Midgley

Illustrated by Beverley Rodgers

THE Second POLITICALLY CORRECT SCRAPBOOK

First published in 2007 by John and Laura Midgley
Trevose House, Orsett Street, London SE11 5PN

Printed and bound in the United Kingdom

ISBN 978-0-9552078-2-2

THE *Second* POLITICALLY CORRECT SCRAPBOOK

As with our first Politically Correct Scrapbook, we have used our artistic licence for this book and whilst virtually everything relates to political correctness, there are a few pieces which perhaps strictly speaking don't but we just could not resist including them!

The actual examples used in this book are either our own personal experiences, the experiences of our supporters or from media reports. To the best of our knowledge, therefore, they are a reflection of real events. We are quite sure that if one or two of the contributions have not occurred exactly as described to us - the way things are going it will only be a matter of time before they do!

Some of the sketches have been taken from the internet or kindly passed to us by our supporters. Where something is 'doing the rounds', for example by e-mail, and there is no known author we have not been able to attribute the work. In these cases we have considerably re-worked the pieces and added illustrations by Beverley Rodgers. We would be delighted, however, to dedicate previously unattributed works and/or correct the sources of quotes if necessary in any subsequent editions of this book. If you have any information to enable us to do this please let us know. We are very grateful indeed to all those who have sent us their stories/ ideas as they have been a great help!

If **you** have any examples of political correctness to share, or come across any amusing pieces which are similar to those included in this book, we would love to hear from you. Please see the back of the book for our contact details.

John and Laura Midgley

We'd like to dedicate this book . . .

It is said that you "learn something new everyday."
Well, I certainly did from my Dad not long before we started to compile this book.

A number of years ago, before my Dad retired as a fire brigade station officer, he came up against the forces of political correctness. He was told that, in the name of "equality and diversity", his brigade had to recruit more women. Anyone who knew my Dad would understand that this was never going to be a problem except that the suggestion was that the criteria was to be altered to enable this to happen.

My Dad felt that this was very wrong especially when you consider that these recruits would be in the frontline saving other people's lives. Dad said that there should be no special favours and that he would only accept women who could, at the very least, do the job as well as the weakest male on his team. I don't think you can say fairer than that!

Sadly, my Dad passed away before this book was completed. We did, however, get the chance to show him some of the chapters which we are really pleased about.

I'd like to take this opportunity to pay tribute to my Dad. He will be sorely missed.

John.

. . . to our Dads!

Where to start? Well, as a clue, this is the only section of this book (and the last book) which will come as a surprise to my Dad! It's the only bit he hasn't been asked to check, double-check and then proof read amongst other things.

Nobody in the family has really escaped when it comes to these books but my poor Dad has been the subject of more phone calls, e-mails, requests, pleas and workload than everyone else put together and multiplied by 100!

The help and support we've received has been invaluable and I can say in all honesty that it would have been very hard indeed to produce these books if it had not been for my Dad.

Some people say, "You can't choose your family.." but I would definitely choose my family any day of the week!

So - for the record - thanks again Dad. We are both very, very, very grateful for EVERYTHING!

Laura

Contents

Contents

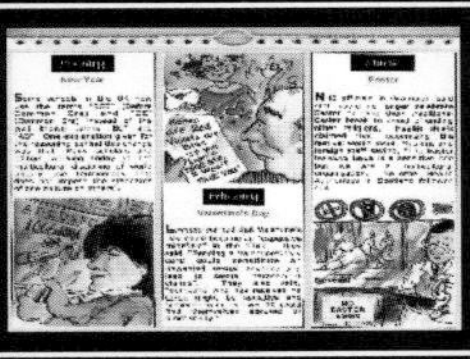

Politically Correct Noah

God looked upon the Earth and saw it filled with wickedness and evil. He decided to destroy it so that he could start again. He picked a man who he knew to be righteous and who he decided should survive. That man was Noah.

God came unto Noah (who had migrated to the UK) and said, “The Earth has become wicked and the end of all flesh is come before me. Make thee an ark of gopher wood. The length of the ark shall be three hundred cubits, the breadth of it fifty cubits and the height of it thirty cubits. A window shalt thou make to the ark; the door of the ark shalt thou set in the side with lower, second and third storeys. I will bring a flood of waters upon the Earth to destroy all flesh and everything that is on the Earth shall die. But then, thee and thy sons and thy wife, and thy sons' wives shalt come to the ark with two of every sort of living thing, to keep them alive with thee; they shall be male and female. I shall come to you in half a year to unleash the floods for 40 days and 40 nights.”

6 months later…

God ordered the skies to become grey in preparation for the floods and came unto Noah.

God looked around but could not see any sign of the ark that he had ordered Noah to build.

“Noah!”, he bellowed, “I have come to unleash the floods to destroy mankind. Where is the ark to save thee, thy family and thy animals?”

"Forgive me", Noah pleaded, "but I have not even started to build the ark."

Thinking he had misjudged Noah completely, God said, "Has thou been idle all this time? Is this the reason the ark is not here before me?"

"Absolutely not", Noah replied, "It is, in fact, quite the opposite."

"Well", said God, "Thou had better start from the beginning!"

"Alright", said Noah, "But you are not going to like this."

"As soon as you left", Noah started, "I got straight to work on the plan of the ark. I did the dimensions as you said in cubits and worked out where the three storeys would go.

I then submitted these plans for Building Regulations Approval to seek permission to build the ark. This was the first stumbling block.

The Local Authority said that they would not accept the plans in cubits and that I hadn't given enough consideration to: fire safety; site preparation; toxic substances; noise insulation; combustion appliances and fuel storage systems; protection from falling, collision and impact; and the conservation of fuel and power.

Whilst I was busy arguing with them I also had to amend the plan to adhere to "The Recreational Craft Regulations 1996" resulting from "The Recreational Craft Directive 94/25/EC" as amended by "Directive 2003/44/EC". These rules cover the ark as they relate to "any craft intended for sport or leisure purposes, regardless of the type or the means of propulsion, with a hull length of 2.5 to 24 metres, measured according to the appropriate harmonised standards". I had to convert everything into metric units, get a builder's plate and write an owner's manual with instructions and information essential for the safe use and maintenance of the ark.

I said that I did not think the floods would keep us in the European Union – rather that they would carry us off elsewhere in actual fact – but I was told that the rules still applied.

Then, whilst waiting for all the approvals to come through, I started trying to find the wood to build the ark. I looked up "gopher wood" on the internet but could not find it so I tried to find a wood that was good for boat making.

Most of the trees locally had tree preservation orders on them to protect bats and owls and I was not allowed to import the wood from the rainforests because they had been declining so much. I pointed out that the world was about to come to an end so this really did not matter but there was no way they were letting me have a twig never mind enough wood to build the ark!

I thought I had better get together the workforce for when the plans came back and the wood was located but this was a nightmare too.

In order to comply with laws on sex discrimination, race discrimination, disability discrimination and age discrimination, I had to interview hundreds of people to prove that I had not discriminated in the recruitment process and that I was committed to so-called “equality and diversity”.

I also had to employ workers on the Construction Skills Certification Scheme with Ark Building Experience and trying to find disabled and female builders with this certificate was no easy task, I can tell you!

In fact, they did not want to do it so I had to pay them double the others **not** to work so that I could put them on my books and prove that I had not discriminated against anyone should I be taken to an Employment Tribunal.

And then there were the animals. Oh God, did I have a problem with the animals! When I started rounding up one male and one female of each species the whole world went berserk.

The Animal Rights Lobby said that I was containing the animals against their will. The council tried to prosecute me for taking badgers under the “Protection of Badgers Act 1992”. Getting the birds was a huge problem as it was illegal under the EU Bird Directive - “79/409/EEC on the Conservation of Wild Birds”.

In order to allow the dogs to breed on board the ark I had to apply for a Dog Breeding Licence under “The Breeding of Dogs Act 1973”.

I also had to get horse passports for the horses and the donkeys under the “The Horse Passports Regulations 2004” from an approved passport issuing agency under “Commission Decision 92/353/EEC” and then had to put them with all our passports to save me from forgetting to pack them!

Under the “Dangerous Wild Animals Act 1976”, as amended by the “Dangerous Wild Animals Act 1976 (Modification) Order 1984”, I could not officially acquire elephants, zebras, rhinos, buffaloes, camels, giraffes, emus, pandas, bears, lions, walruses or tigers so this caused some problems - especially when I had to try and coax them out of the zoo.

Once I had rounded up the animals I had to prove that they would be kept in accommodation which prevented their escape; which was suitable in respect of construction, size, temperature, drainage and cleanliness; where the animals would be supplied with adequate and suitable food, drink and bedding material; and be visited at suitable intervals.

I also had to show that I had taken appropriate steps to ensure the protection of the animals in case of fire or other emergency.

Then, when the Equalities Body received a complaint from a couple of gay goldfish who had heard that I was only taking one male and one female of each species they charged me with discrimination against animals in same sex relationships and took me to court.

I explained that I had to have one male and one female so that they could reproduce but was told that this amounted to “Prohibited Discrimination” and I now have a criminal record for the first time in my 600 year life!

And, finally, when Customs and Excise got wind of the project, they came to seize all my assets.

They rounded up the animals saying they had reason to believe that I was going to leave the country illegally with endangered species.

I said that I wasn’t technically leaving the country as the country was about to cease to exist.

I also said that I was actually trying to protect the animals as all species were now endangered because the earth was about to be destroyed but they still took them all away.”

Suddenly the skies cleared and the sun started to shine. A huge bright rainbow could be seen across the sky.

Noah looked up in wonder and said to God, “Does this mean you are not going to unleash the floods and destroy the world?”

“No, I am not going to unleash the floods”, said God.

Noah looked quizzically at God and said, “But why have you changed your mind?”

God replied, “Because the world appears to have been destroyed already!!”

The End

What It Means To Be British

**People are always asking what it really means to be British.
Well, we think we've cracked it! Being British is about....**

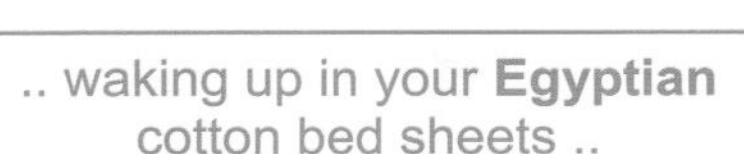

.. waking up in your **Egyptian** cotton bed sheets ..

.. to the buzz of your **Taiwanese** alarm clock ..

.. getting dressed in your **Chinese** made clothes ..

.. splashing on your **French** perfume or aftershave ..

.. drinking your **Kenyan** coffee ..

.. with **Danish** bacon for breakfast ..

.. then checking your **Swiss** watch ..

.. before setting off for work in your **German** car ..

.. having lunch at an **Italian** restaurant ..

.. and a cup of **Sri Lankan** tea back at the office ..

.. popping to an **Irish** pub after work ..

.. for a **Belgian** beer ..

.. then using your **Korean** mobile phone ..

.. to call for an **Indian** takeaway ..

.. or going home for **New Zealand** lamb ..

.. washed down with some **Australian** wine ..

.. ending up relaxing on your **Swedish** sofa ..

.. with a tipple of fine **Portuguese** Port ..

.. and a big fat **Cuban** cigar ..

.. watching **American** TV programmes ..

.. on your **Japanese** TV!

And the most British thing of all?

Suspicion of anything foreign!

MADE IN JAPAN
WELCOME TO LAS VEGAS NEVADA
MADE IN CUBA
MADE IN PORTUGAL
MADE IN SWITZERLAND
MADE IN CHINA
MADE IN KOREA
MADE IN SWEDEN
B

The Politically Correct Lord's Prayer

The Politically Correct Lord's Prayer

Our Father (or Mother, Step Father, Step Mother, Carer or Guardian) who art in the non-denominational resting place

Inclusive be thy name

Thy persondom come, thy will be done

On earth as it is in the non-denominational resting place

Give us this day our daily burger and coke

And forgive us our trespasses

As we are forced to forgive those who trespass against us by illegally camping on land and refusing to move

And lead us not into temptation

But deliver us from those who are not politically correct

For thine is the persondom, the power of thought control and the glory of human rights

For ever and ever

Aperson

Politically Correct Stories

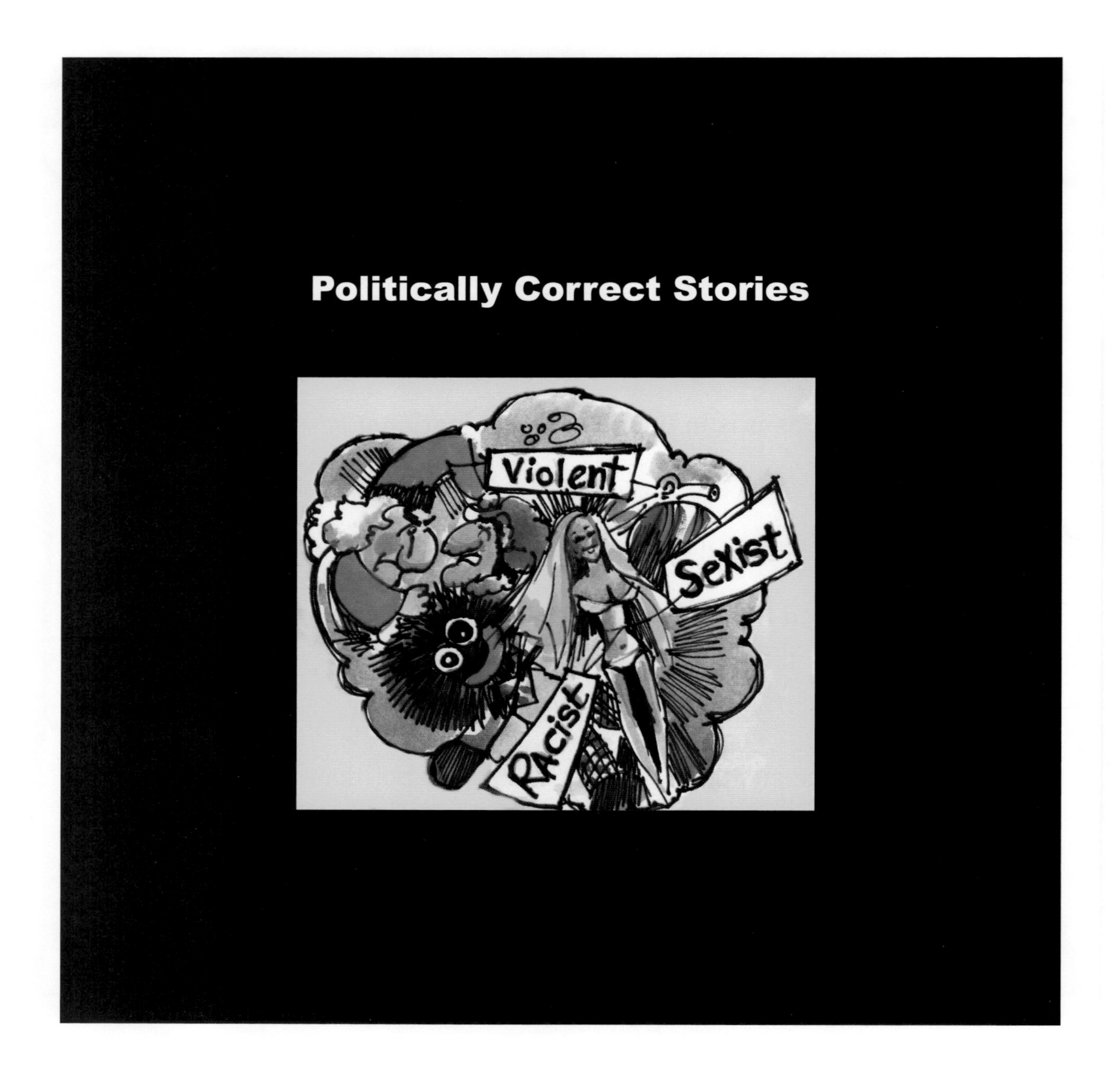

Politically Correct Times

A Government website (www.direct.gov.uk) listed advice for Britons going to live abroad. It said "Understanding a country's laws and customs can help you adjust to a new home abroad" and "Appreciating cultural and legal differences could also help you avoid potentially embarrassing or difficult situations." It then went on to give suggestions as to how to fit into a new country saying "Get a good guidebook and find out about local laws, customs and culture, ideally learn the local language and at least take a phrase book; respect local customs and dress codes; think about what you wear and how you fit in; be discreet about your views on cultural differences; behave and dress appropriately and take particular care not to offend Islamic codes of dress and behaviour." No such advice was issued to entrants to the UK.

Employees of a Government Agency were sent on a two-day crash course to learn Urdu and Hindi. Some weeks later they were conducting a survey and, at one house, the occupants were Indian. The senior manager, who had been on the course, insisted that the survey was conducted in broken Urdu (adding considerably to the time taken) despite the fact the Indian couple spoke perfect English and said they would prefer to give the interview in English.

A 19 year-old woman who had passed written tests to join the police was asked in her interview what, on joining the force, she would do if she needed advice. When she answered, "I would go to my sergeant and ask him for help" she was failed for referring to the sergeant as "him" and thereby "showing a lack of gender awareness".

Police visited a shop in Lancashire after a woman complained about the sale of golly dolls. Officers arrived and confiscated one 6 inch doll and one keyring. They took a statement from the shop owner and told him to remove the remaining gollies. The police were eventually forced to conclude that no offence had been committed and the dolls were put back on sale.

Politically Correct Times

A teacher was given training material for her class on the Government's Skills for Life syllabus which said, "Meet the Singh family. Mr Singh is a good Hindu and goes to the temple every week. Meet the Mahmouds. Mr Mahmoud is a good Muslim and prays 5 times a day. Meet Mrs Baker. Mrs Baker is divorced and has 2 children and does not go to church." Mrs Baker was the example chosen for the "typical white Brit".

After an investigation by Ofcom following one complaint about a scene from a Tom and Jerry cartoon, which showed Tom smoking during a momentary break from the endless violence, the Boomerang Channel agreed to go back through its library of Tom and Jerry cartoons and edit out scenes which could glamorise or condone smoking. No suggestion was made that the violence should be toned down in any way.

The Egg Information Service was told by the Broadcast Advertising Clearance Centre that they would not be allowed to screen 50 year-old adverts featuring Tony Hancock and eggs. The old adverts encouraged people to "Go to work on an egg" and did not, according to the Advertising Authority, encourage a "balanced diet".

The Scotland Yard Museum - the "Black Museum" - was renamed the "Crime Museum" after a police officer complained about the use of the term 'Black' in the title.

The new owners of the "Fat Louis' Bar" on the Grand Parade in Skegness decided to rename it "Busters" because some people found the old name offensive.

The Governor of a large prison threatened one of his employees with disciplinary action and forced him to issue a written apology after the employee ran a light-hearted piece in the prison newsletter with a play on words. The piece contained alternative word meanings and the "offensive" terms were apparently: '*retard* - something really hard in North Yorkshire' and '*debasement* - de room under de floor.'

Politically Correct Times

The Union Flag did not fly from Bournemouth Town Hall for the Queen's official 80th birthday. Apparently no staff were available to hoist the flag as her birthday fell on a Saturday. Yet, a few weeks later, the Gay Pride flag was flown from the Town Hall over a weekend to coincide with the Bourne Free Gay Pride Festival, which also fell on a Saturday.

Scouts at their centenary celebrations on Brownsea Island were given vegetarian food and sat around a pot plant instead of a fire. A spokeswoman for the Scout Association said, "It was really to do with religion that we were not able to provide sausages and burgers and all that kind of food. We have been very careful to make sure food is provided to everybody's tastes and beliefs, so no-one feels left out."

Tower Hamlets Council caused a furore on Bonfire Night by having a party with no guy and no bonfire. Members of the public were treated instead to a £75,000 fire show in the local Victoria Park re-telling a Bengali folk tale about an emperor and his tax collectors. When questioned about this bizarre move, a spokesman for the Council said, "We did Guy Fawkes last year!".

A council in Barking shut down a lift which was used by the elderly and the infirm for one week to add Braille buttons to the control panel. They did not seem to think it odd that the only destination for the lift was a car park and not much use to blind people who clearly don't drive. Any blind people going to a car would only be doing so with someone who would be driving and who would, therefore, also operate the lift.

David Clutterbuck, a councillor in Bournemouth, was told that he should apologise and go on equality training after saying that, in light of all the new laws and rules about equality, if Noah was building his ark today it would no doubt be "illegal to only have animals of the opposite sex" in order to reproduce after the world had been destroyed.

Politically Correct Times

A Deputy Headmaster was astounded to be told by a local authority that he could not place an advert for a new teacher using the words 'dynamic' and 'enthusiastic' as they were deemed to be "ageist". Many were at a loss to understand why it was not possible for anyone of <u>any</u> age to be 'dynamic' and 'enthusiastic' and thought that perhaps it was the authority that was being "ageist" for suggesting otherwise.

A lengthy memo told staff at South Lanarkshire Council to avoid words like 'mankind', 'manpower' and 'office girl'. Also ruled unacceptable were the words 'Mrs', 'Miss', 'love', 'pet' and 'dear' as the council said, "Women do not need to reveal marital status through using Mrs and Miss. This practice is sexist and discriminatory. Use of discriminatory language may be subject to disciplinary action or may lead to dismissal".

The word "Yob" was banned from reports submitted to the Metropolitan Police Authority after it appeared in the phrase "proactively tackling gangs and yobs across London". The Authority's Deputy Chairman, Cindy Butts, objected to its use saying, "I have a problem with the language of 'yobs'".

A company who wanted to advertise for a qualified German speaker to provide written translations was told by the local Job Centre that it could not use the term 'mother-tongue' in the advert as it was "gender-specific, discriminatory and not inclusive". Instead, the company was told that they would have to use the expression "native speaker or near-native equivalent".

The pipe traditionally smoked by Sherlock Holmes (which was used as a measure in terms of how many pipe-loads of tobacco it took to solve a case) was banned from the programme, 'Sherlock Holmes and The Baker Street Irregulars' shown on the BBC. They said, "Ofcom has strict guidelines on what you can and can't show on children's television. Smoking should not be condoned, justified or encouraged".

Politically Correct Times

A fireman with 15 years experience faced disciplinary action after jumping into the River Tay in Perth to save the life of a woman who was drowning. Fire chiefs admitted that the fire engines were not equipped with the correct poles and ropes to save the woman but that brigade rules state that fire personnel should not enter the water. The fireman said he had a choice of watching the woman die or taking action as she was losing consciousness and the rescue rope his crew had been using had snapped.

The headteacher of Johnstown Primary School, in Carmarthen, West Wales, banned the making of traditional Mother's Day cards at the school because she said it could be seen as insensitive to the five per cent of the pupils who did not have mothers.

Police in Cheshire visited an 11 year-old boy at home after he allegedly called a schoolfriend 'gay' in an e-mail. His mother (a magistrate) said she was amazed when the police turned up and thought at first it was a joke. Cheshire Police said, "The use of the word 'gay' would imply this is homophobic but we would be hard-pushed to say this is a homophobic crime".

The term 'purdah' - long used by civil servants to describe the period leading up to an election when no politically contentious announcements are made - was banned during the Welsh Assembly elections in case it offended Muslims and other religious groups. Apparently, in Persian, 'purdah' literally means "curtain".

A TV programme recreating a scene from the 1960s showed a nurse saying, "You'll just feel a little scratch", instead of "You'll just feel a little prick".

A Detective Constable faced disciplinary action after calling a career criminal "pondlife". He was told that if the criminal had heard what had been said he "might have been offended".

Politically Correct Times

A 2 year-old boy was banned from a shop in York for wearing a hood. The shop had a "no hoods" policy and refused to make any exceptions.

A secondary school teacher told a pupil that they should no longer refer to "trial and error" and should now use the phrase "trial and improvement" because the former was too negative.

The daughter of the man who created the Dandy's best-loved character, Desperate Dan, 70 years ago said that the changes made to the character over the years were "completely ridiculous" and that her father would be horrified if he could see the modern Dan. The character used to be huge, shave with a blowtorch, part his hair with a pistol shot and munch cow pie (including the horns and tails) but now he is slimmer, much less butch and has a water pistol instead of a gun.

An internet chat group campaigning for a medication to be made widely available to treat hypothyroidism was closed down after one person complained that their logo was offensive. The logo was of a little smiling pig and had been chosen simply because the medication came from pigs.

Staff running a crematorium in Nottinghamshire were told they would have to replace the 40 memorial benches in their grounds at a cost of £200,000 in order to comply with new Disability Discrimination legislation. The benches, which had been bought by friends and relatives of the deceased (and used in some cases for many years), were measured and found to be 3 inches lower than the minimum height necessary to comply with the new legislation.

The Headmaster of a London primary school changed his title to "Lead Learner" saying, "I want to show pupils that learning is not something that stops when they leave school and that even as adults there is still plenty to learn. So I see this new title as a better reflection of my role and purpose".

Politically Correct Times

A teenage science student was told she could not apply for a training programme with the Environment Agency because she was white and English. The position in the Anglia region was advertised with a £13,000 per year tax free grant and the Environment Agency's job vacancy notice said, "Applications are encouraged from people of the following descents: Asian, Indian, White other (e.g. Irish, Welsh, Scottish, European), African, Caribbean or of Mixed Race origins." After sending an e-mail asking for clarification, the student was astounded to be told that as she was white and English she would not be considered for the position, even though it would have been perfect for her. She said, "I really wanted to work for the agency....I would not have minded had I been beaten for the position by somebody better able than me."

A hotel manager who deputised as the number caller on a Bingo Night refused to read out what he called the "offensive non-PC terminology" common in Bingo games such as "Two Fat Ladies (88)" and "Legs Eleven (11)".

Displays on the fronts of buses on a circular route in Harrow were changed to show just the destination - 'Harrow'. The route each particular bus used was not shown because, apparently, the writing on the bus advising the main stops on the way was deemed not to be accessible to the "sight impaired". Officials failed to grasp, however, that, as a consequence, nobody knew which bus they were getting on and where it was going - other than its final destination - which was exactly the same for the buses going in both directions!

Norfolk County Council advised Headteachers in the area that they should not encourage sniffer dogs and their handlers to visit their schools in case the dogs found drugs. The person in charge of Children's Services said that if drugs were found on a pupil, "It would lead to that child being highlighted or bullied" and said that this would be "unfortunate on the child".

Politically Correct Times

A nursery in Surrey taught the children to sing a less upsetting version of Humpty Dumpty which went:

"Humpty Dumpty sat on a wall. Humpty Dumpty had a great fall.

Humpty Dumpty opened his eyes. Falling off was such a surprise!"

A 54-page report entitled 'Fair For All - The Wider Challenge - Good Lesbian Gay Bisexual and Transgender (LGBT) Practice in the NHS' (written by a group with funding from the NHS in Scotland and backed by gay rights activists) suggested that the NHS should have a zero tolerance approach to staff who used discriminatory language such as 'mother and father' and 'husband and wife'. Instead it said they should use phrases like 'guardians' or 'carers' and 'partners' or 'close friends'.

The Royal Society for the Protection of Birds' website banned the use of the word "cock" on its online forum, when used to describe a male bird, and replaced the word with four asterisks. It did not, however, edit the word "tit" used for the female of the species.

A woman who asked for a Life Assurance quotation was told that her premium had increased slightly to take into account information supplied on the application form (which had not been known when the telephone quotation had been given). When the woman asked why this was, she was told that it was because of her "height/ weight ratio". The woman asked if it was because she was considered "fat" or "overweight" and was told that these were not words the Insurance Company employees were allowed to use.

A woman went into a jewellers shop to buy a crucifix on a necklace for her mother's birthday. However, she was told that the shop no longer stocked crucifixes because they believed they were offensive to Muslims.

Politically Correct Times

A woman who was completing an online form for the police, reporting some credit card fraud experienced by the company she worked for, was surprised to be asked her race and height. The information was classed as compulsory and she was not able to enter the statement on behalf of her company unless she included these details.

Philip Meeson, who runs the low cost airline Jet2.com, was accused of being racist after he posted a picture of a frog lazing around during a strike by French Air Traffic Control workers. The strike had affected many airline passengers and caused flight chaos. When an interviewer told him that he should not have used the words "lazy" and "frog", Mr Meeson said, "I can. I have".

The 30 year-old tradition of "conger cuddling" which had raised large amounts of money for the Royal National Lifeboat Institution (RNLI) was forced to end after someone complained about the use of a dead fish in the competition. The event in Lyme Regis, Dorset, had been a huge local attraction but it was criticised for being disrespectful for encouraging teams to use a dead eel in the competition to try to knock members of other teams off their flower pots. The winning team had been the one with the most members on their pots at the end after the swinging of the 25lb eel. Local organisers said that the RNLI had advised them that they were "not prepared to be involved in an event that may be seen by some to be a barbaric throwback due to its use of a dead animal."

The name of a flotation device used at a pool in Scotland was changed from "Woggle" to "Noodle" so as not to cause offence.

A woman on a course at a Further Education College in Kent, who said that she had been "dropped on her head as a child and had never been the same since", was warned by her tutor not to "make light of disabilities".

Politically Correct Times

Councillor Paul Scully who called 'works of art' in St Helier's, Surrey, "totem poles" (because of their shape) was told by the Mayor of Sutton that he should not use the phrase "totem poles" as it could be offensive to Native Americans. Mayor Myfanwy Wallace said, "I wonder if the indigenous people who designed totem poles would wish you to call it a totem pole".

A baker was told by Dorset County Council's Trading Standards department to re-name her novelty cakes which had animals and birds on top because they said "Food must be properly described so consumers can tell what it is". Val Temple, who had been selling her 'Robin and Pig Tarts' for 16 years to happy customers was told she had to change the names of the cakes as they did not contain pigs or robins. A farmer was also told that he could no longer label his sausages "Welsh Dragon Sausages". A spokesman for Powys Council said, "The product Welsh Dragon Sausages was not sufficiently precise to inform the purchaser of the true nature of the food. I don't think anyone would imagine that dragon meat was being used but we would not want vegetarians to buy the sausages believing them to be meat free."

The BBC was accused of watering down the famous prison comedy 'Porridge' in a repeat of the programme by removing a comment about the camp chef character 'Lukewarm' played by Christopher Biggins. In one of the repeat episodes, a reference to how tidy 'Lukewarm's' prison cell was kept was edited out allegedly to avoid offending homosexuals. Christopher Biggins said, "I find it quite extraordinary. It was always so well done, the gay thing."

A policeman looking for car thieves (who had fled from a stolen car and were thought to be hiding in some gardens near a house in Bexleyheath) told the homeowner that he, his 5 colleagues, their police dog and police helicopter were looking for "Bla..." suspects but stopped himself before finishing the sentence with "...ck".

Politically Correct Times

Despite being over budget, the organisers of the London 2012 Olympics advertised for 10 members of staff on salaries of up to £100,000 each plus bonuses to deal with "equalities". One of their priorities was to make sure there were sufficient numbers of female and ethnic minority construction workers. The jobs included a 'Head of Equality and Inclusion'; a 'Deputy Head of Equality and Inclusion'; an 'Equality Monitoring and Research Manager'; an 'Equality and Inclusion Manager (Audit and Support)'; and an 'Equality and Inclusion Manager (Impact and Engagement)'.

Police in Burnham on Sea told a group of five year-olds that they could not chalk squares on the playing area in their cul-de-sac in order to play hopscotch as it was considered to be "graffiti".

A firm in Walsall in the West Midlands was not allowed to place an advert in their local Job Centre for an assistant who spoke German to deal with a particular client as they were told this would unfairly discriminate against those who could not speak German!

The Managing Director of Drusillas Park in Alfriston, East Sussex, was told by his legal human resources advisers that he could not discriminate by advertising for a fat 'Fat Controller' to run the park's Thomas the Tank Engine train ride. This was despite the fact that staff had gone to enormous trouble to make sure the theme ride was an exact replica of the books and the television programme. He was told that he would have to interview a thin person if they applied for the job even though he wanted a genuinely 'fat' Fat Controller for authenticity.

A couple were told that they would not be allowed to foster children as the husband had "indicated a lack of understanding..a negative attitude towards Eastern Europeans". The man had been delayed on route to the 4-day fostering course and all he had said was that he had been held up on the way because of an "accident involving four foreigners".

Politically Correct Times

Staff at a bakery in Kidderminster told those asking for "gingerbread men" that they no longer sold "gingerbread men" but could offer a "gingerbread person" instead.

The cross worn by Fiona Bruce on the BBC's 10 o'clock news was criticised by a former controller of editorial policy at the BBC. He said that wearing the cross whilst reading the news was a mistake.

A series of books recommended by a campaign called 'No Outsiders' have been used in schools in the UK to help children as young as 4 address "lesbian, gay and transgender issues". The books are called 'And Tango Makes Three' (the story of two male penguins in Central Park Zoo who bring up a penguin chick); 'King and King' (about two princes who fall in love); & 'Spacegirl Pukes' (about a space-travelling girl with two mums who gets a tummy bug). One teacher said, "We had read King and King [as part of our literacy work on altering traditional tales]. We began the lesson with a letter from the Prince asking the class for help because he has to meet all these princesses but didn't want to marry any of them. The children then had to make puppets of their own Cinderella characters. Lots of boys decided to have male Cinderellas."

Police in Greater Manchester were banned from using the word 'Township' because it was considered racist. A police inspector deemed the word unsuitable and issued a memo to his staff saying that the term was barred. In Rochdale, the term was removed from official letterheads, notepaper and signs in five police stations within the division. The irony was that it was the police themselves who had introduced the word 'Township' and had even created 'Township Inspectors' only a year earlier.

Firemen were banned from letting children sit in fire engines during school visits and community events in Devon because it was feared that the firemen could be accused of "touching up" the children as they lifted them up and down.

Politically Correct Times

Organisers of a 30 year-old annual summer festival in Primrose Hill were told they would not get a £400 grant from Camden Council unless they: 1) Made sure that five per cent of festivalgoers filled in a questionnaire to say whether they had enjoyed themselves; 2) Invited 'under-represented groups' to participate as stall-holders or performers; 3) Hired only professional caterers who registered with their local authority; 4) Made sure all staff, artists and volunteers had a Criminal Records Bureau (CRB) check; 5) Used only a gas barbeque.

A Home Office Review recommended that Immigration Officers should not wear their standard issue navy blue uniforms when deporting illegal immigrants and should instead wear "clothing in softer colours".

A Buddhist businessman who wanted to call his Chinese restaurant in Durham the 'Fat Buddha' was told by the local council that, "To use the name of a major religion's deity runs contrary to this city's reputation as a place of equality and respect for others' views and religious beliefs." They said the name was "inappropriate in a city founded on faith" and that they didn't "want to offend anyone". They also said the council operated "a strict non-discriminatory equal opportunities and diversity policy across the board". The stunned restaurant owner said, "The fat Buddha is a symbol of health and happiness". A spokesman for the Buddhist Society said, "Buddhists regard the fat Buddha as lucky. To suggest this is offensive is to misunderstand the faith. Buddhists don't take offence at anything because to do so doesn't follow Buddhist teachings."

A man who was well qualified for a job as an ambulance man was turned down after interview because of a "lack of diversity and equal opportunities knowledge". He was told that he had been unsuccessful as he had been unsure of the answer to give when asked the protocol for attending an emergency call at a mosque.

Politically Correct Times

To avoid falling foul of Age Discrimination Legislation, staff in offices all over the UK were told not to celebrate birthdays by putting up 'Happy 40th/50th etc Birthday' banners or balloons and not to put candles on birthday cakes which in any way referred to an employee's age.

Church of England guidelines for bishops and priests blamed the "uncritical use of masculine imagery" for encouraging men to behave violently towards women and said that the clergy should reconsider the language they used. It went on to say, "Many conceptions of God derived from the Bible and the Christian tradition have portrayed divine power in unhealthy and potentially oppressive ways. There are particular problems in the attribution of violent actions and attitudes to God, chiefly but not solely in the Old Testament, which require careful interpretation." The guidelines also said, "The 'post-Christian' feminist Mary Daley had a point when she said in the 1970s, 'If God is male, then the male is God'. Church teaching and preaching must correct this major imbalance."

A little girl came home from school and said that she had been learning how to write letters. The mother asked her daughter to show her what she had learnt and the little girl started writing "i am...". The mother said, "Weren't you taught to use a capital 'I'?" The little girl said they did not do that as it implied they were more important than the person being written to. She said they had been taught to use a small 'i' at all times.

An Access Course student who wanted to become a teacher was told she would not need a Science GCSE because she was born before 1979. Yet, in the middle of her course, she was told she would have to have this qualification after all because Age Discrimination Legislation meant she could no longer be exempted purely because she was a student of a certain age - as had been the case in the past.

Politically Correct Times

A man with a business based near a large council estate agreed to sponsor a Kids' Fun Day, because it was felt the local community would benefit from the involvement of nearby businesses. The business representatives attended a meeting with a council employee who informed them that the day would be known as a "Multicultural Kids Fun Day". When the businessman pointed out that this would imply the kids on the estate were all different, he was told that it was the council's aim to celebrate "diversity" and that every opportunity should be used to promote it.

A woman who suggested using the Union Flag as part of a graphic for a nationwide promotion, to advertise the fact that the business she worked for was UK based, was told that this "may offend some people".

Thames Valley Police recruited two 16 year-olds as Police Community Support Officers saying, "They reflect the community in which they serve, that includes all ages, genders and races". Many members of the public were, however, very concerned about this in light of the fact that the role of a Police Community Support Officer includes the following: providing support for front-line policing, conducting house-to-house enquiries, guarding crime scenes, providing crime prevention advice, issuing fixed penalty notices for many offences (including anti-social behaviour), group dispersal, directing traffic, removing vehicles, detaining someone until a constable arrives, requiring someone to give their name and address, searching for and seizing alcohol from people drinking in the street (and from under 18s) and seizing drugs.

Instructors at a police training centre in a remote part of rural England were told not to use the words "Wagon" or "Wheel" in case they caused offence to "Native Americans" (or Indians). They were told that, back in the 1800s, "Native Americans" had been tied to a wagon wheel and so the phrase could upset them if they ever attended the training centre.

Politically Correct Times

A lecturer who went to a fancy dress party dressed all in black as a piece of coal was told by his boss that his outfit had been "racially hostile". Photographs of the event were posted by someone else on the faculty's internal website and, when they were seen by the lecturer's boss, he was told he would have to undergo "cultural sensitivity training" at work to keep his job.

Two families who had lived next door to each other for over fifteen years and had always been close fell out one day after a heated argument. The argument occurred because one family accused the other of having a "racist" dog, after the dog had barked at their daughter's new boyfriend who was black. Apparently, the evidence that the dog was racist was that it was normally well-mannered and friendly towards everyone.

A student group which sent round an e-mail to arrange a gathering, mentioned that there would be "bacon rolls" available at the event. The University's Equality and Diversity Department intervened and said that, whilst they could eat bacon rolls (which were in fact sold at the canteen), they could not refer to them in the e-mail in case this caused offence.

A man who worked alongside people with severe learning difficulties was told on a course that he should never say "Out of my mind" because this could be offensive to the people he worked with. After pointing out that the people he helped had very little grasp of the basic language and that they were a tad unlikely, therefore, to be offended by the nuances of phrases such as this, he was subjected to a ½ hour lecture about the need to be politically correct at work.

Hampshire Police force bosses sent uniformed police officers on skateboarding workshops alongside local youngsters in an effort to make the officers look 'cool'. The point of the exercise was to "break down any negative attitudes towards the police" amongst youngsters in the area.

Politically Correct Times

An e-mail which was sent to hundreds of thousands of customers was rejected by several County Council e-mail addresses as it contained the name of the (apparently racist) flower "Black Violet".

The Rev Alan Barrett, the vicar of St Editha's Church in Tamworth, Staffs, and a father of three, said he was left with little choice but to resign as Chairman of Governors of William McGregor Primary School on the advice of the Archdeacon of Lichfield after he gave a 10 year-old girl a congratulatory peck on the cheek when he presented her with a certificate in front of fellow pupils and a maths teacher. The girl's mother complained but investigations by the police, social services and the Church all cleared the Reverend Barrett of doing anything wrong.

A man in Middlesbrough who had his wheelie bin stolen was offered counselling from Victim Support. He received a letter offering him "emotional support and practical help" over his missing wheelie bin.

A woman, working for a University as a temp, referred to a man from China as a 'Chinaman'. Her Head of Department gave her a severe telling off for being racist. When she asked her boss why this was racist seeing as 'Englishman', 'Frenchman' and 'Scotsman' were commonly used phrases, her boss just got more irate.

A child's passport photo was rejected by a Post Office worker on the grounds that the child's bare shoulders were just in the picture and this could be offensive to Muslims.

Trevor Phillips, Head of the Equality Commission said the country would face "stormy times" if history was not written to be more "inclusive".

An Aberdeen NHS newsletter asked staff not to dress their children (who used the staff crèche) in witch t-shirts, costumes or badges at Halloween time in case it "offended real witches".

Politically Correct Times

An organisation called 'Family Links', which promotes 'relationship skills' in families, said that parents should not call their children "naughty" or send them to sit on a "naughty step". It said that doing so put the parents and children in a really different, and much more antagonistic, mindset.

Cookery courses in a prison to teach inmates basic cooking skills were stopped after 15 years because a Race Relations Liaison Officer said that the course was disadvantaging prisoners from a 'BME' (ethnic minority) background. Although it was pointed out that the recipes used covered a wide range of ethnicities and that a degree of discipline was essential for the prisoners to learn anything, the Race Officer said that it was not good enough as the "learners" could not choose to cook their own thing.

An old man went into a hospital, gave his name for an appointment, said that he was 'crippled' and asked if the staff could bear this in mind when dealing with his case. The receptionist turned to the old man and said, "You can't call yourself crippled".

The driver of a holiday coach arriving at Calais was asked if he had any non-EU passport holders onboard. When he replied "Yes", he was told that all the passengers on the coach would have to alight and go through a formal immigration procedure, even though 34 out of 38 were British passport holders. When he asked why the British passport holders had to go through this procedure, when their passports were normally checked on the coach and no further paperwork was needed, he was told "some people think it's racist to only ask the foreign passport holders to get off the coach".

A Scotsman wrote to a local newspaper in Hampshire, after the paper launched a campaign for pride on St George's Day, saying that the idea would cause "division" and "intimidate minorities".

Politically Correct Times

When the term "Women Police Constables" was dropped as a police title, and "WPCs" became known simply as "PCs", several police forces in England went through their websites and changed thousands of references from "WPC" to "PC" retrospectively. When asked whether they thought this was a good use of police time, one force said that it might have been a "bit excessive".

A woman who had a tongue-in-cheek sign outside her cottage for more than 30 years saying "Our dogs are fed on Jehovah's Witnesses" was told by police to take it down because it could be deemed to be a "hate crime". The sign had been put up after Jehovah's Witnesses called on the house repeatedly but local Jehovah's Witnesses confirmed it didn't cause offence.

Fire chiefs in Knutsford said that they would not give any more press stories to the local paper, the Knutsford Guardian, until it stopped using "sexist" language by referring to "Firemen" in their articles. The newspaper's editor, Sue Briggs, said that she would not back down but would give the final say to the people of Knutsford. The result of a poll, undertaken over the course of a month, was a resounding 73.3% in favour of using the term "Firemen". As a result, the newspaper vowed to continue using the term in their articles.

Teachers at a school in Manchester refused to send out a letter to the parents of a child who had lice (and who regularly passed the lice on to other children) as they did not want to "cause offence".

A woman who was asked to enter a password for a website chose the word "fairycake" only to be told by the system that she could not have this password because it was "offensive". Apparently the word "fairy" had triggered this reaction as it was included on a list of words which could be offensive - in this instance to homosexuals.

Politically Correct Times

A retired major who had served with the King's African Rifles during the Second World War was told he could not send old pictures of members of African regiments, which he had kept, to a 12 year-old Zambian boy he was sponsoring. The charity he paid his sponsorship to, said the photographs were "unsuitable for the child" adding they had "a policy not to pass on letters, photos and other gifts depicting images of war."

A row broke out after some ethnic groups in Southall complained about the use of bilingual signs at Southall railway station. The signs had been displayed in English and Punjabi but other local ethnic groups said that the use of just Punjabi as an additional language was discriminatory. They demanded equal rights for all languages. However, First Great Western said, "...it would be impossible to provide station signage for every language".

A couple visiting their daughter and her new baby in Aberdeen Royal Infirmary, who asked staff whether their daughter's husband had yet arrived, were rebuked for saying the word "husband" which was, apparently, viewed as derogatory. They were told they should use the term "partner" instead.

Tower Hamlets Council advertised the job of "Hate Crime Policy and Partnership Manager" for a salary of £39,738 - £42,231. The advert said the Council had "a strong commitment to equalities and community cohesion, having achieved level 5 of the Equalities Standard and Beacon Status for promoting racial equality and community cohesion." The advert was placed at the same time as it was revealed that public libraries in Tower Hamlets stocked books by Abu Hamza and other convicted fundamentalists and that there were more fundamentalist texts than moderate books on their shelves. Eight libraries in Tower Hamlets were found to contain several hundred books and audiotapes by radical Islamics which glorified, incited and endorsed acts of terrorism against those of other religions, as well as endorsing violence against women.

Politically Correct Times

The editor of a parish magazine felt he had to resign after including a few Irish jokes in one edition of the magazine. Cornwall County Council's Head of Equality and Diversity Service had complained about the use of the names "Paddy" and "Murphy" in the jokes, saying they ridiculed the Irish traveller community with whom she worked. She wrote to local schools asking them to boycott the publication so as to avoid their articles being "published alongside such derogatory material". Her letter also said that the jokes "...use racist language or ridicule based on race as defined under the Race Relations (Amendment) Act 2000 and which may have an impact on the attitude and behaviour of children". The editor, Mr Lusby, who had spent 11 years building up the magazine, was actually Irish himself and his middle name was Patrick - Paddy for short!

A pioneering Christian course offered to inmates in Dartmoor Prison ended as it failed to comply with the prison's diversity policies. Those running the Christian course said they had been told to teach a bit of every religion or they would not be complying with the "multi-faith" agenda.

A girl aged 5 was asked at Sunday School who Jesus loved. After saying, "Mum" and "Dad" she said, "and Mrs Herritt". The Sunday School teacher asked the girl, "And who is Mrs Herritt?" to which the girl replied, "She's a black cow" - as she was, in fact, one of the Aberdeen Angus cattle owned by parents. Her mother was then accused of being racist and of teaching her daughter to be racist. She was asked to refer in the future to the black cows as "brown animal friends" and not to use either of the words "black" or "cow", in case they caused offence.

A Minister of a church in Dudley was amazed to be told by council officials that, in order to erect a cross in the grounds of his church, he would have to pay a £75 fee. This was because the cross was deemed to be an "advert" as defined in the Town and Country Planning Act 1990.

Politically Correct Times

The Forestry Commission ordered a study to investigate the 'under-representation' of women in the British Forestry Industry. The research was to identify the issues faced by women foresters and to explore the reasons why women were 'under-represented'. The report blamed the butch "lumberjack" stereotype in forestry for this - clearly they wanted more "lumberjills" instead!

A school in Scotland changed the numbers of its classes from 1A and 1B in case those in class 1B felt inferior to those in class 1A - despite the fact it was quite clear that the make up of the two classes was based on the dates of birth of the pupils.

Avon and Somerset Police were criticised for displaying signs in text message format in Bristol centre. One message read, "D bil cum arnd hre n wl vzit ur olds if ur messin bout" which could have read "The police patrol this area and if you are acting in an anti-social way be sure that they will tell your parents". Another sign read "Du ur olds knw whr u r o wot ur doin coz D bil wl tel em" which could have simply said "Do your parents know where you are or what you are doing because the police will tell them".

A row broke out in Didcot after Council Leader Cllr John Flood forwarded a poem about different colours of skin. The poem read: "Me coloured? When I born, I black, when I grow up, I black, when I go in sun, I black, when I scared, I black, when I sick, I black, and when I die, I still black...And you white fellow, when you born, you pink, when you grow up, you white, when you go in sun, you red, when you cold, you blue, when you scared, you yellow, when you sick, you green, and when you die, you grey... And you call me coloured?". Former Council Leader, Cllr Margaret Davies called the poem, "racist, offensive and abhorrent". Cllr Flood, however, pointed out that it was nothing of the sort and that Dr John Sentamu, Archbishop of York, had in fact used the poem in his address at his installation as Chancellor of York St John University!

Politically Correct Pub Names

The SAD but TRUE Times

"Off With His Head"

Vicar calls for "offensive" pub name to be changed

A vicar in Birmingham said that his local "Saracen's Head" Pub should be renamed, as the title was "offensive". Despite protests from the local community, the vicar still maintained that the name was "clearly disrespectful" to Muslims. However, a local Muslim Doctor said, "It's not offensive – it means nothing to me" and a local Muslim student said, "I don't find it offensive and I don't think anyone of my age would".

John Midgley, Co-Founder of the Campaign Against Political Correctness, said, "If we had to change all the pub names in the UK that could be considered offensive, it would be a very long job. Presumably they would call 'The Two Chairmen' sexist; 'The Midget' offensive to little people; 'The Trafalgar' - too patriotic; 'The Old Albert' ageist; and is 'The Punch and Judy' too violent? Whatever next?".

TO

BLACK DOG
PUB

TO

MULTICOLOURED
DOG
PUB

THE
TRAFALGAR

TO

THE
LOVE BOAT

THE TWO CHAIRMEN
•PUB•

TO

THE TWO CHAIRS
•PUB•

THE OLD ALBERT

TO

THE AGELESS ALBERT

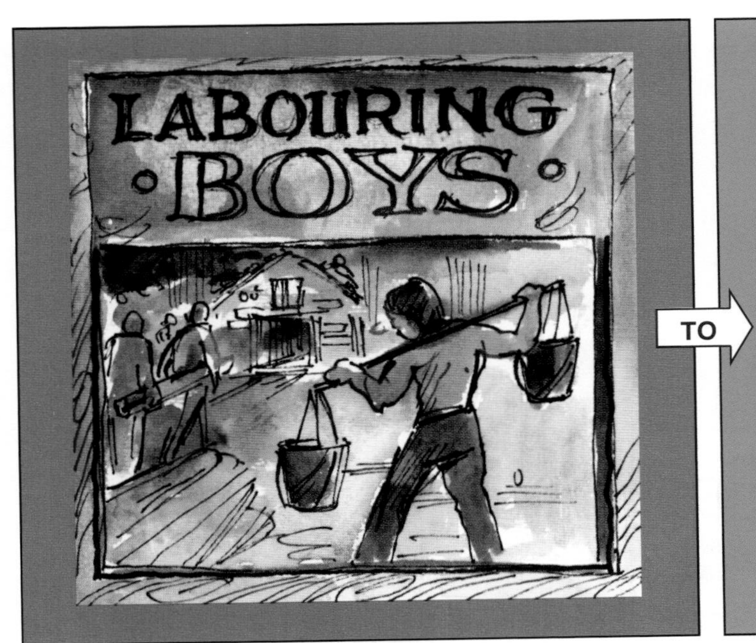
LABOURING
BOYS

TO

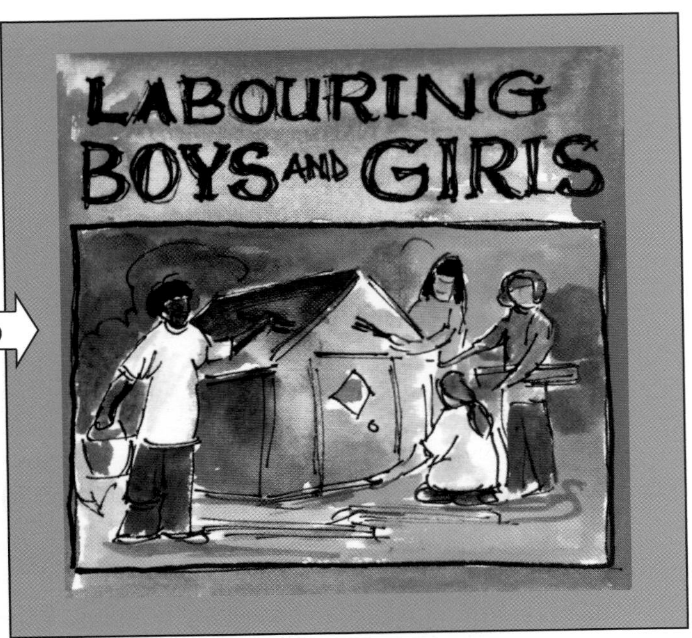
LABOURING
BOYS AND GIRLS

THE
PUNCH & JUDY

TO

THE
PACIFIST & JUDY

"Ageist" Jokes

"Employers also have to make sure ageist jokes are banned as they could lead to harassment claims. ACAS says the rules would even cover the situation where a father and son worked in the same office and the son took offence at ageist jokes aimed at his father. And it adds that it would be "good practice" to make sure customers and suppliers did not make ageist jokes as well." **Extract from the '*Daily Telegraph*' on Age Discrimination Legislation in Britain.**

The one about sharing everything....

A young man was watching an elderly couple in a pub one lunchtime. He noticed that they ordered one meal and an extra cup.

As he watched, the gentleman carefully halved the sandwich then counted out the chips, dividing them into two piles. Then he poured half of the coffee into the extra cup and set that in front of his wife.

The old man began to eat and his wife sat waiting.

Feeling a little awkward, the young man walked over and offered to buy a meal so they could have one each.

The old gentleman said, "Oh no. We've been married for 50 years and we always share everything 50/50."

"Well", said the young man to the old woman, "do you mind me asking why you're not eating yet?"

"Not at all", she said, "it's his turn with the teeth!"

The one about the name....

Two very elderly ladies had been friends for over 70 years.

One day they were playing cards when the first old lady looked at the second old lady and said, "Now don't get mad at me.....I know we've been friends for a long time.....but I just can't remember your name! I've racked my brains but it has just gone - I can't think what it is. Can you please remind me what it is and I promise I won't forget it again?"

The second old lady glared at the first old lady for a long time with a deeply furrowed brow. Eventually she said, "How soon do you need to know?"

The one about the Hokey Cokey....

The man who wrote "The Hokey Cokey" died peacefully at home.

The most traumatic part for his family was getting him into the coffin.

They put his left leg in... and then the trouble started!

The one about living to 80....

Edgar (aged 75) recently had a complete health check. His doctor said he was doing "fairly well" for his age.

A little concerned about that comment, Edgar couldn't resist asking the doctor, "Do you think I'll live to be 80?"

The doctor asked, "Well, do you smoke or drink beer, wine or spirits excessively?"

"Oh no", Edgar replied, "I've never done that."

Then the doctor asked, "Do you spend a lot of time in the sun, perhaps playing golf?"

"No, I don't", Edgar replied.

“Do you eat a lot of nice but fatty foods”, the doctor said.

“No, I eat very healthily”, said Edgar.

Then the doctor asked, "Do you gamble, drive fast cars or have lots of fun with women?"

"No", Edgar said, "I don't do any of those things."

The good doctor looked at Edgar and said, "Then why the heck do you want to live to be 80?"

The one about the wedding....

Albert (aged 89) and Mary (aged 87) were very excited about their decision to get married. They were in town buying a few bits and pieces for their wedding when they went past a Boots chemist. Albert said he had just had a bright idea and wanted to go in.

He said to the man at the pharmacy desk: "Do you sell heart medication?"

Pharmacist: "We do indeed."

Albert: "How about medicine for circulation?"

Pharmacist: "All kinds."

Albert: "Medicine for rheumatism?"

Pharmacist: "Definitely."

Albert: "Medicine for memory?"

Pharmacist: "Yes, a large variety."

Albert: "What about vitamins and sleeping pills?"

Pharmacist: “Absolutely."

Albert: "Perfect! We'd like to register here for our wedding list please!"

The one about the wife falling out the car....

An elderly man was heading home in his car one evening when he was stopped by a policeman.

"Are you alright, Sir?", the policeman said after the gentleman had wound down his window at the roadside.

"I think so", the man replied, smiling, "why do you ask?"

"Sir, I am afraid that I have to tell you that your wife fell out of the car about a mile back."

"Oh, thank goodness", the man exclaimed, "I thought I'd gone deaf!"

The one about going to the club....

Fred (aged 82) still thinks of himself as a ladies' man. Every Friday night, he dresses up smartly, slicks down his hair and heads off to his favourite club.

When he gets there, he walks up to the bar, sidles up to the prettiest girl he can find and says, "So, tell me, do I come here often?"

The one about golf....

Two old men decided that they would play a round of golf.

When they got to the first hole, one of the old men said to the other, "My eyesight isn't what it used to be - can you watch my ball for me and tell me where it lands?"

"Of course", says the other old man, "my eyesight is fine - go ahead and take your shot."

The first old man steps up to the tee and whacks the golf ball into the distance. He turns to his friend and says, "Did you see where that went?"

"I certainly did", says the other man.

"Where is it then?", said the first old man.

The second man thinks for a minute and then says, "I am sorry mate - I can't remember!"

The one about being 104....

A reporter was interviewing an 104 year-old woman. "What do you think is the best thing about being 104?", the reporter asked. The old lady replied, "No peer pressure!"

The one about the wrinkles….

Philip and his wife were getting ready for bed when his wife said to him, "You know, I look in the mirror and I see an old woman. My face is all wrinkled, my chest is barely above my waist. I've got varicose veins and my arms are so flabby they look like wings."

She turns to Philip and says, "Come on, tell me something positive to make me feel better about myself."

Philip thinks about it for a bit and then says in a soft voice, "Well…..there's clearly nothing wrong with your eyesight!"

The one about the peacock….

An old man was observing a teenager sitting at a nearby table in a café.

The teenager had spiked hair in all different colours: green, red, orange, and blue.

The old man kept staring at him. The teenager would look over every so often to find the old man looking at him every time. Eventually, the teenager went over to the man's table and asked him sarcastically, "What's the matter old man, never done anything wild in your life?"

The old man said, "Oh yes. I got drunk once and had a relationship with a peacock. I was just wondering if you were my son!"

The one about the hearing aid….

A man said to his neighbour, "I just bought a new hearing aid. It cost me £3,000 but it's state of the art. It's fantastic. I don't know how I ever managed without it before."

"Really", answered the neighbour, "what kind is it?"

"1 o'clock!"

The one about the heart….

93 year-old Ethel decided that she wanted to go out in style having had a good innings in life. She thought that an old Army pistol would be the quickest way and planned to shoot herself in the heart. Not wanting to miss the vital organ, she called her doctor's office to enquire exactly where her heart should be. She was told it would be 'just below her left breast'.

Later that night Ethel was admitted to hospital with a gunshot wound to her knee!

Old Age - Personal Ads

FOXY LADY: Smart, fashion-conscious blue-haired beauty, 80's, slim, 5'3" (used to be 5'6"), searching for sharp-looking, sharp-dressing companion. Matching socks preferable.

WINNING SMILE: Active grandmother with original teeth seeking grandfather with own teeth to share rare steaks, corn on the cob and caramel sweets.

LONG-TERM COMMITMENT: Recent widow who has just buried fifth husband looking for someone to help fill a six-unit burial plot. Dizziness, fainting, shortness of breath not a problem.

MEMORIES: I can usually remember Monday to Thursday. If you can remember Friday, Saturday and Sunday, let's put our two heads together.

PEACE NOW: Into solitude, long walks, sunrises, the ocean, yoga and meditation. If you are the silent type, let's get together, take our hearing aids out and enjoy some quiet times.

GOOD CONDITION: Male, 1932, high mileage, some hair, many new parts including hip, knee and teeth. Not in running condition, but walking well.

Modern Day Fable

THE ANT AND THE GRASSHOPPER

THE ORIGINAL VERSION

The ant works hard in the withering heat all summer long, building and improving his house and preparing supplies for the winter.

The grasshopper thinks the ant is a fool and laughs, dances and plays the summer away.

Come winter, the ant is warm and well fed.

The shivering grasshopper has no food or shelter - so he dies, out in the cold.

THE MODERN DAY VERSION

The ant works hard in the withering heat all summer long, building and improving his house and preparing supplies for the winter.

The grasshopper thinks the ant is a fool and laughs, dances and plays the summer away.

Come winter, the ant is warm and well fed.

The grasshopper has no food or shelter.

However, alerted by a social worker who finds the shivering grasshopper, his plight becomes the top news story.

Live TV coverage is shown of the grasshopper on the streets - cold and starving.

This contrasts with video footage of the ant in his warm, comfortable home and his table laden with food.

The newsreaders encourage people to vote in their daily poll about whether or not this sort of situation is acceptable in “Modern Britain”.

The press write stories about how we should be ashamed that, in a country of such wealth, this poor grasshopper is allowed to suffer in this way.

The Grasshopper Council of Great Britain is hopping mad and demonstrates against such unfairness in front of the ant's house as well as outside Parliament, demanding that the Government introduces a law to prevent this discrimination.

The ant's taxes are then increased to cover the cost of subsidising the grasshopper and also to pay for a new "equality" body, the Commission for Grasshopper Equality, to prove that the Government will not tolerate discrimination against grasshoppers in any form.

The Commission for Grasshopper Equality is given a huge budget to investigate why grasshoppers are poorer than ants, less qualified than ants, have worse housing than ants, are more likely to live in deprived areas than ants, don't hold as many senior positions in business as ants and are not represented in Parliament in the same numbers as ants.

When the ant suggests that this has nothing to do with discrimination and is actually down to the grasshopper's lifestyle choice, he is forced to go on a course on "Species Awareness".

He is "taught" never to make the same, highly inflammatory, offensive "speciesist" comments again.

The grasshopper is then provided with a free council house and money to furnish it.

The Government launches an “Equality and Diversity Plan for Grasshoppers” and prosecutes the ant’s business for failing to employ enough grasshoppers. The ant points out that no grasshoppers want to work for his firm but this is not accepted as a satisfactory explanation.

The grasshopper gets bored watching his free TV all day so he starts hanging around with some grasshopper mates on the corner of the street.

As the ant scuttles to and from work, they laugh and jeer at him making him feel unsafe in his own neighbourhood. They also play their music loud late into the night so that the ant cannot get to sleep and is tired for work the next day.

The ant’s taxes go up again to pay for the grasshopper’s house and he wonders if he will be able to survive.

A documentary is shown on television of the “poor” bored grasshopper having nothing to do all day.

With a shot of the grasshopper wearing a hoodie and lurking in a corner the voiceover says:

“It’s no wonder that the grasshopper prefers to stand around on a street corner all day as he has absolutely no facilities anywhere near his home.”

The programme concludes, *“The Government must do more to provide entertainment and sports for poor grasshoppers who live in some of the most deprived parts of the country and end this social exclusion now!”*

Then, bored of tormenting the ant every time he passes, the grasshopper decides to burgle the ant's house. Whilst the ant is out at work, the grasshopper breaks down the ant's front door and pinches his things. The grasshopper thinks he will sell the ant's things on the street as it will save him waiting for his benefits to come through.

However, he is caught red-handed by the police. The grasshopper tells the police that he did not mean to steal the ant's things and is very sorry.

He is not sent to prison because the legal aid lawyer, who the ant paid for through his taxes, says it is his client's "Grasshopper Rights" not to be sent to prison.

Leading grasshopper rights activists talk about the phenomenon of a "grasshopper underclass" and say that the grasshopper just needs a bit of love.

Whilst continuing his crusade of victimising the ant, the grasshopper decides it would be fun to try some drugs.

When a policeman catches him with some grass, the grasshopper is let off with a caution as he says it is just for his personal use.

He quickly becomes addicted to hard drugs and a vast network of support is given by social services, health teams and charities.

Again, the ant's taxes go up to fund these schemes.

The grasshopper continues to rob more and more ants to feed his drug habit. After being arrested for one particularly nasty attack, he is held in prison overnight.

However, the prison warders do not respect his right to vegetarian food and give him small insects to eat. So he is let out of prison immediately and given a huge compensation settlement for his hurt feelings and the distress caused.

Meanwhile, his girlfriend (a teenage grasshopper) gives birth to the couple's fifth baby grasshopper and the whole family are moved as a priority to a bigger house around the corner.

There is an issue about the paternity of the second and third grasshopper babies but this is resolved when the couple go on TV and have a DNA test.

With his (taxpayer funded) compensation windfall, the grasshopper is able to buy all the drugs he wants for him and his grasshopper mates.

Eventually he has too many drugs for his body to cope with. He overdoses and dies.

Having spent all his money on illegal drugs, there is nothing left, so the hard working ant's taxes have to go up yet again to provide continuing support for the grasshopper's family.

The grasshopper's death is blamed on the failure of Government to address the root causes of despair arising from social inequality and deprivation in Britain.

More money is committed to the Commission for Grasshopper Equality as the drug problem is thought to be widespread amongst grasshoppers but not ants.

Politicians want answers as to why this should be; they insist there can be no justification for this unacceptable difference in “Modern Britain”.

The Commission for Grasshopper Equality launches its “Grasshoppers’ Charter”.

The Charter is designed to tackle the “deep seated causes and symptoms of social exclusion and create cohesive, thriving, sustainable communities with a view to ending deprivation and disadvantage.”

The ant decides he has had enough of this psychobabble and politically correct nonsense.

He packs up his remaining belongings and books a cheap flight to Spain.

He is quite sure that he will be able to live a better, more prosperous life in Spain …. and he sincerely hopes there won’t be any lazy grasshoppers around over there!

The End

Health and Safety Stories

Health and Safety Guardian

After an inspection by Cheshire County Council's Rights of Way Officer, Macclesfield Borough Council was told to remove some goalposts used by children from one of their fields. This was in case walkers using the footpath across the field fell over them whilst their heads were bent down reading their maps.

Telephone operators at the Vale of Glamorgan Council in Barry, South Wales, no longer answer the phone in English and Welsh because union officials were concerned that saying, "Bore da" or "Prynhawn da" could strain their vocal chords. The union said that cutting down on the time spent speaking, by dropping the extra phrase, would comply with recommended health and safety advice for good practice at call centres.

Children were banned from taking part in the annual donkey derby in Llandudno in North Wales where they had previously been able to ride on the donkeys during the 30-second races. Initially parents had been asked to sign a disclaimer form to allow their children to participate but, after Insurers refused to cover the event, the children's places were taken by inflatable sheep and a stuffed orang-utan. The local Mayor said, "It's very sad to see it's got to the stage that children are not allowed to enjoy themselves. It is only a few donkeys running around in a circle, not the Grand National".

Staff at swimming pools in Bournemouth were told they could no longer lend inflatable armbands to children in case someone picked up an infection when blowing them up.

Police dogs in the North Wales Police Force were muzzled to prevent them from causing injury to criminals. The dogs were trained to stop suspects or disarm them using their heads instead.

A parent was sent a letter requesting permission for his son to participate in his school's "tasting of shop-bought scones, cakes and pies".

Health and Safety Guardian

Children were banned from using jumpers as makeshift goalposts in a cul-de-sac in Leicestershire after they were described as a "danger to the public".

Children at Burnham Grammar School in Buckinghamshire were told that they could no longer play football during breaks to ensure that people were not hit by stray balls.

The National Blood Service stopped giving donors hand grips at blood donor sessions. They said there had never been a problem with the grips used by donors to help them to give blood but cleaning and disinfecting the grips was not now, apparently, satisfactory from a health and safety point of view. The National Blood Service blamed, "an age of increasing regulation driven by Europe and the UK" and said they were "increasingly required to minimise risks". As a result, donors were left with little option but to simply dig their fingers into their palms without the comfort of the grips. Donors complained that this was risky and painful. However, this was not a major concern to the Service as donors provided their own fingernails and the Service could not be sued if there was a problem.

Roadside speed indicators worth more than £100,000 were found to be lying unused in Lancashire because council workers had not been trained to climb ladders. The thirty-six Speed Indicator Displays (Spids), to warn drivers about speeding, had been bought by parish councils but were not erected as ladders had to be used to install them. Under health and safety laws people needed to be trained to operate ladders before they could use them for any purpose.

The Government was warned that because police manuals had become so heavy (weighing 2½ lbs) they "could be used as weapons". Transferring the manuals onto compact discs for use with a computer was, however, deemed not to be an option as CD roms were classed as items which could be used by vulnerable people to harm themselves.

Health and Safety Guardian

Three firemen from Bury were investigated for their "involvement in the use of unauthorised rest facilities". Their crime was to sleep on the floor in sleeping bags during their rest periods rather than to use the risk assessed reclining chairs provided for them. The chairs had been supplied at a cost of £130,000 and all staff had to undergo health and safety training before they were allowed to use them. Some firemen preferred not to use the chairs and carry on as they had done prior to their arrival.

A community annual festival in Hartlepool (attracting more than 2,000 participants each year) was forced to drop the sack race, the three-legged race and the egg and spoon race from the event as the cost of insurance cover for these races alone more than doubled the existing premium.

A man who decided to do the gardening in his communal garden area (which had been neglected by the local council) was served a notice by Oxfordshire Council's Crime and Nuisance Action Team. He was banned from mowing the lawn, making compost and painting doors in the communal area despite the fact that his neighbours were all happy with the work he was doing. He was also told he had to have the written consent of any neighbour in the sheltered accommodation if he subsequently ended up helping them and a copy of the consent had to be lodged with the council.

Lights were left on in a disused school near Edinburgh as council bosses said they had a "duty of care" to protect people entering the school - even if they were burglars or vandals!

A woman who rang the police to report that her handbag had been stolen was told that the operator could not make a report of the incident. This was because the headset on their telephone was not working and internal health and safety rules meant they were not allowed to use the telephone handset and write at the same time.

Health and Safety Guardian

A Sheffield clown known as "Barney Baloney" was forced to stop blowing bubbles for children to chase because it was deemed a safety hazard. He was also banned by a supermarket from blowing up balloons and shaping them into animals. A spokesman for the supermarket said, "This is a health and safety issue. We have banned balloons because latex is used in the manufacture of them".

A "Welcome" sign in an Edinburgh suburb, which had been vandalised, was deemed too unsafe to clean without first stopping the traffic, removing it and taking it away. Despite the fact that the sign was only 8 feet high and on the pavement, council officials took no action for over a year prompting one local to say, "I can reach it if I stand on my tip-toes. It would be a ten-minute job". Having made some enquiries, he said he would buy a special aerosol anti-graffiti can and a sponge, costing less than £10, use his ladder and clean the offending vandalism himself.

Big yellow signs were erected in estate grounds under some huge oak trees, which had been around for hundreds of years, warning people not to sit under the trees as something might fall on them.

A Health and Safety Inspector ended the door-step postal service of a hamlet in Wales after identifying 23 hazards capable of inflicting major injury to the postman on the route - despite the fact there had never been any injuries. One of the most worrying obstacles was identified as a stile opposite Bettws Farm, near Abergavenny. Under the heading "Harm Potential" the report stated: "Risk of slip/trip/fall resulting in muscle/tendon strains or broken bones, cuts, grazes, and bruising". Another major concern was a local farm identified as a "working farmyard with a muddy surface, loose stones and a raised cobbled area". The report warned users of possible "collision with farm vehicles or machinery" and said that drivers could "lose control of their vehicles". The probable severity of these incidents was listed as "fatal".

Health and Safety Guardian

Residents in Wiltshire were told they could not pick up litter (as a group) without first applying for a licence. Residents of Urchfont had won the best-kept village competition several times and villagers were always keen to work together to keep the place clean and tidy. Going out on their own was apparently fine but special health and safety requirements came into force if there was a group of people. Not long before this, a 79 year-old resident had been told that she could not weed flower-beds in the village unless she wore a high visibility jacket and displayed "men at work" signs around the flowerbed for the duration of her gardening.

A 3 year-old girl was banned from using a float at a swimming pool in Exeter in case she hurt herself with the polystyrene block.

A man who had flu and went into his local chemist to buy a thermometer was told that he would have to purchase a digital one. He could not be sold an 'old-style' one for health and safety reasons as it contained mercury.

A bench erected to enable elderly passengers to rest whilst waiting for buses at a bus stop in Stoke-on-Trent was built facing away from the road and towards a hedge. Council officials said that they had made the decision as some elderly passengers were "unsteady on their feet" and this positioning would be "less dangerous". However, local elderly passengers said that not only was it patronising in the extreme but they had to crick their necks just to see if the bus was coming because they were sitting facing the wrong way!

A charity 'bunny hop' in North Wales had to be cancelled as organisers could not afford the £600 insurance cover in case any of the participants injured themselves. In previous years the event - which saw up to 75 adults and children dressed as rabbits with floppy ears and fluffy tails race 200 yards along a course through the town - had raised money for a local hospice.

Health and Safety Guardian

Police did not chase a thief making off on a moped as he was not wearing a helmet and they feared being sued if the thief fell off and injured himself. Avon and Somerset police later said that aborting a pursuit because the rider was not wearing a helmet was one of the "options available" to officers when "members of the public or the riders themselves could be put in danger".

All the tree roots and the grass areas around rabbit holes were painted with white paint on and around a well worn path in Steyning in West Sussex to stop people from tripping over.

A woman was told she had to remove the angels and cherubs she had placed at the side of her husband's grave in Brockworth, Gloucestershire, in case anyone injured themselves on them and sued the council.

A 10 year-old girl told her mother that she needed to take some items to school for a project and they had to be recycled. When the mother put the middles of toilet rolls (as she had done before) into her daughter's bag, the girl said she had been told she could no longer take the toilet rolls into school "for hygiene reasons".

A council in Somerset ordered allotment holders to take out Public Liability insurance for £5 million at a premium of £375 per head each year as the allotments were considered a risk. The annual allotment fee was only £10.

Toys were removed from the waiting rooms of two Preston doctors' surgeries because of health and safety fears. A notice in the reception areas, signed by the practice manager, told patients: "Due to health and safety regulations and the possibility of cross-infection, we are unable to provide any toys or books for children in the waiting room".

Funeral directors were forced to ask mourners to sign a disclaimer if they wanted to carry a coffin with a heavy corpse inside for "health and safety reasons".

Health and Safety Guardian

A Health and Safety Executive research team based at the Health and Safety Laboratory in Buxton, Derbyshire, spent nearly a month and £12,000 investigating "The Role of Towels as a Control to Reduce Slip Potential". The work involved testing towels placed on tiles and other surfaces to re-create bathroom scenes where a towel is placed on the floor instead of a bathmat. The report finally concluded: "Unfortunately the testing carried out here is insufficient to draw significant conclusions".

A fire station was built without the traditional pole for fears that firemen could sprain their ankles as they hit the ground. Officials said a lack of space and health and safety regulations meant that it would be better for the firemen to run down the stairs instead.

Signs were displayed in the Health and Safety Executive's offices nationwide saying, "Do not lift tables or chairs without giving 48 hours notice to HSE management" after an internal assessment of the "risks of manual handling".

When a lollipop man went off sick, the local council refused to allow anyone else to take over. The council said, "A series of rigorous checks and training procedures is in place to ensure that anyone employed to carry out crossing patrol duties meets a number of requirements". They sent a letter to parents saying that they should not help either because, as individuals, they would be personally liable for any accidents. The pupils (as young as seven) were left to dodge rush-hour traffic on their own.

A woman in her sixties was told that she could not buy alcohol from a supermarket in West Kirkby in the Wirral without providing some identification. Jackie Hall was shocked to be asked for ID to confirm that she was over 21 before being allowed to buy a bottle of gin. The supermarket apparently had a policy of asking everyone for ID regardless of how old they looked.

Health and Safety Guardian

A man who had been an auctioneer for 40 years received a letter from Worcester Health and Safety Executive asking him to prove that his voice was not excessively loud. They said, "After receiving a complaint from a member of the public about the noise levels at Hereford Poultry Market, we have written a series of letters to the auctioneers". They also asked how often in the week, staff were exposed to clucking chickens.

Officials at Ilfracombe Rugby Club decided to organise a 'virtual' bonfire to replace the real thing on Guy Fawkes night after previously cancelling the event. They had been put off by the mountain of paperwork and the regulations set by the local council. Recorded images of a roaring fire were projected onto a 16ft by 12ft screen on a scaffolding stand. Giant heaters, lighting, smoke machines and fire crackling noises from speakers were used to try to give the feel of a real bonfire night.

Members of the public in Devon were banned from a local school's summer fête because of the 'risk' they could pose. The fête made very little profit as no members of the public had been able to go along and contribute to the fund-raising effort.

Organisers pulled the plug on a 'Bath Tub Race' in Shoreham, East Sussex, after it had taken place for 35 years and raised £250,000 for charity the previous year alone. The race had involved cast iron tubs being decorated, made seaworthy and then rowed for 6 miles along the River Adur. The Bath Tub Race Committee Chairman said, "It's a whacky race which has generally been great fun but increasing health and safety requirements, insurance rates and other problems mean this kind of activity is no longer viable".

The author of a book honouring First World War soldiers was told he would have to stump up £150 for an insurance premium before his book could be sold by the Tourist Information Centre in Swindon. This was "to provide accident cover in case a member of the public injured themselves on the book".

Men and Women
very, very different

Women. Men. Very Very Different. Equal.

Adam was walking around the garden of Eden feeling very lonely, so God said to him, "What's wrong Adam?"

“I am lonely God, here on my own. I have nobody to talk to”, Adam replied.

God said, “In that case I shall create a companion for you and it will be someone called a ‘woman’. This woman will gather food for you, cook for you and, when you discover clothing, she'll wash it for you.”

God carried on, “She will always agree with every decision you make. She will bear your children and never ask you to get up in the middle of the night to take care of them.”

Adam was listening intently as God continued, “She will not nag you and will always be the first to admit she was wrong when you've had a disagreement. She will never have a headache and will give you love, support and passion whenever you need it."

Adam said to God, "So, what’s the catch? What is all this going to cost me?"

God replied, "Well, it will cost you an arm and a leg."

Adam thought for a minute looking at his arm and leg then said, "Mmmm. Well, what can I get for a rib instead then?"

The rest is history.

Men - not possible to get it right?

If a man asks a woman to do something she doesn't want to, it's domination.
If a woman asks a man to do something he doesn't want to, it's a favour.
If a man doesn't keep himself in shape, he is a slob.
If a woman does not keep herself in shape, people say that fat is beautiful.

If a man has a boring job with repetitive work and low pay, he should get a better job.
If a woman has a boring job with repetitive work and low pay, it's exploitation.
If a man gets a promotion ahead of a woman, it's sexism.
If woman get a promotion ahead of a man, that's equal opportunities.

If a man buys flowers, he must be up to something.
If a woman does not get any flowers, she feels neglected and unloved.
If a man is a househusband, he is a pansy.
If a woman is a housewife, it's totally sexist and the hardest job in the world.

The Advantages of Being a Man

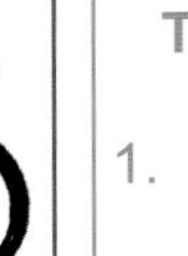

1. Wrinkles add character.
2. One mood - all the time.
3. Car mechanics tell you the truth.
4. Your last name does not usually change.
5. Wedding plans take care of themselves.
6. A week-long holiday only requires one bag.
7. You can open all your own jars.
8. You can sit in silence watching a match.
9. You know which way to turn a bolt.
10. Christmas shopping can be done in one go.

The Advantages of Being a Woman

1. Free drinks.
2. You can choose your own clothes.
3. Chocolate really can be the answer.
4. You can quickly end an argument by crying.
5. You know your glass by your lipstick mark.
6. Shops are everywhere if you need therapy.
7. The 'glass ceiling' is to blame for everything.
8. You can pinch other people's desserts.
9. Speeding tickets - what are they?
10. You are never wrong.

THE FEMALE BOOK OF SPOOF RECORDS

Car Parking—The smallest kerbside space successfully reversed into by a woman was one of 19.36m (63ft 2ins), equivalent to four standard parking spaces, by Mrs Elizabeth Simpkins, driving a Volkswagen Polo with power steering. She started the manoeuvre at 11.15am in Romsey, Hampshire, and successfully parked within three feet of the pavement 8 hours 14 minutes later. There was slight damage to the bumpers and wings of her own car and two adjoining cars (as well as a shop frontage and two lampposts) but the car was definitely parked!

Group Toilet Visit—The record for the largest group of women to visit a toilet simultaneously is held by 147 workers at the Government's Social Security Department, Longbenton. At their annual Christmas celebration at a night club in Newcastle Upon Tyne, Miss Cheryl Crabtree got up to go to the toilet and was immediately followed by 146 other members of the party. Moving en masse, the group entered the toilet at 9.52pm and, after waiting for everyone to finish, emerged 2 hrs 37 minutes later with a further 36 friends whom they had picked up during the trip!

Shop Dithering—The longest time spent dithering in a shop was 12 days by Mrs Sandra Wilks in the Birmingham branch of Dorothy Perkins. Entering the shop on a Saturday morning, Mrs Wilks could not choose between two near identical dresses which were both in the sale. Her husband, sitting on a chair by the changing room for the first day with his head in his hands, told her to buy both. Mrs Wilks eventually bought one after 12 days of agonising. Mrs Wilks also holds the record for window shopping, when she stood motionless gazing at a pair of shoes on display in nearby Jones the Bootmakers for 3 weeks and 2 days!

Jumble Sale Massacre—The greatest number of old ladies to perish whilst fighting at a jumble sale is 98, at a Church Hall in Baildon, West Yorkshire. When the doors opened at 10.00am, the initial scramble to enter cost 16 lives, a further 25 being killed in a crush at the first table. A seven-way skirmish then broke out over a pinafore dress costing 10p which escalated into a full scale melee resulting in the loss of another 18 lives. A pitched battle over a headscarf then ensued and quickly spread throughout the hall, claiming another 39 old women. The jumble sale raised £5.28 for the local boy scouts!

Single Breath Sentence—A Lancashire woman became the first to break the thirty minute barrier for talking without drawing breath. Mrs Mavis Sommers of Leigh, Lancashire, smashed the previous record of 23 minutes when she excitedly told her neighbour about an argument she'd had in the bakers. She ranted on for a staggering 32 minutes and 12 seconds without pausing for air. At that point she went blue in the face and collapsed in a heap on the ground. She was taken to Leigh Infirmary but was released later after check-ups. At the peak of her mammoth motor-mouth marathon, she achieved an unbelievable 680 words per minute, repeating the main points of the story 114 times and going off on 82 different tangents!

Gossiping—Joyce Blatherwick told her close friend Agnes Banbury, in the strictest confidence, that she was having an affair with the butcher. After Mrs Blatherwick left at 2.10pm, Mrs Banbury immediately began telling villagers - swearing them all to secrecy. By 2.30pm that day, she had told 128 people the news. By 2.50pm, it had risen to 372 and by 4.00pm that afternoon, 2,774 knew of the affair, including the local Amateur Dramatic Society, several knitting circles, a coachload of American tourists and the butcher’s wife. When a tired Mrs Banbury went to bed at 11.55pm that night, Mrs Blatherwick's affair was common knowledge to a staggering 75,338 people!

THE MALE BOOK OF SPOOF RECORDS

Injuries before seeking medical treatment—The man who had the most injuries before eventually seeking medical treatment was Mr Bert Johnson from Accrington who was injured in the first instance by a wayward cricket ball. Despite the appearance of a lump the size of a molehill on his forehead, Mr Johnson claimed that it was "absolutely nothing". On his way home, he fell over a stray cat and broke his leg. Insisting that he was "fighting fit" to concerned passers-by, he limped on only to fall down an uncovered manhole. Despite breaking both arms in the fall, he continued on his way. It was only, finally, when a police car ran over his toes and broke them, he conceded that he possibly might need a plaster or two for his injuries!

TV Remote Flicking—Mr Dirk Davidson from Manchester holds the record for flicking through the 71 channels on his TV in the quickest time. Returning from work one day, Mr Davidson commandeered the remote control which his wife had previously been using and managed to absent-mindedly flick through all the channels in just 13 seconds without registering what was on any of them!

Preparation for a Father's race—The record for the most training done before a Father's race at a children's sports day is held by Mr Kurt Philpott of Cambridgeshire who started training as soon as his son was born. By the time of his son's first sports day he had racked up 2,912 hours of training. Meeting other fathers at the starting line on the long awaited race day, he was dressed head to toe in the latest aerodynamic sports gear. Allegedly arriving "straight from the office", he pretended that the race was of no consequence at all - "just a bit of fun". Yet, he had, in fact, taken the day off work and had been warming up in a nearby field - timed to perfection - to maximise his performance!

DIY Danger—The most men involved in DIY accidents in one place was on an August Bank Holiday Monday in Hatch Warren, Basingstoke. The local branch of B&Q reported record sales of DIY equipment in the morning. Fire engines and ambulances became a regular sight on the estate that afternoon. One of the victims was Mr Roger Vaughan who had been trying to fit a shelf which he had bought 3 years earlier. He slipped in the middle of the operation involving "No More Nails" and found himself covered in the entire tube. The fire brigade had to remove him from this very sticky position and then attended a staggering 32 similar DIY incidents within 2 hours!

Driving Behaviour—The record for the most number of insults towards other drivers in the shortest space of time is held by Mr Mark Forth who, whilst out on a 35-minute drive from Liverpool to Chester, managed to gesticulate and shout at 247 passing cars. According to Mr Forth, who shouted non-stop throughout the entire journey, all the other drivers he passed along the way were useless and should be taken off the road forthwith!

Longest Distance Driven Whilst Refusing To Ask For Directions—The record for the longest distance driven whilst refusing to stop and ask for directions on a trip which was only "round the corner" is held by Mr Matthew Ford. He popped out in his car with Mrs Ford in the morning to find a local supermarket 3 streets away whilst on holiday in Southend-on-Sea. Taking an early wrong turning, Mr Ford soon found himself on the road to Rayleigh and then failing to take the right road back to Southend-on-Sea travelled on to Basildon reaching South Ockendon an hour later. Ignoring his wife's advice to simply stop and ask someone the way, things took a further turn for the worse when he managed to join the M25 by accident and then ended up in the Dartford Tunnel. He eventually arrived back at his holiday apartment 13 hours 43 minutes after leaving. As his weary wife crawled out of the car, Mr Ford said he was delighted at "having found a new way to the shop", which he was convinced nobody else had ever tried!

Anytown Bank decided to install a "Drive-Through" cash point machine to speed up the process of withdrawing money and sent the following instructions to its customers depending on their sex.

MALE PROCEDURE

1 Drive up to the cash machine.
2 Wind down your car window.
3 Insert card into machine and enter PIN.
4 Enter amount of cash required and withdraw.
5 Retrieve card, collect cash and receipt.
6 Wind up window.
7 Drive off.

N.B. If you find yourself in the queue behind a woman, it is suggested that you buy a cup of coffee from the conveniently located "Drive-Through" coffee shop next door. When you return she might just about be halfway through the procedure, allowing you the rest of the time to enjoy drinking your coffee!

FEMALE PROCEDURE

1 Drive up to cash machine.
2 Reverse back the required amount to align car.
3 Restart the stalled engine.
4 Wind down the window.
5 Find handbag and remove all contents on to passenger seat to locate card.
6 Turn the radio down.
7 Attempt to insert card into machine.
8 Open car door to allow easier access to machine due to the wide gap.
9 Insert card.
10 Re-insert card the right way up.
11 Search through contents of handbag again to find diary with PIN number on back page.
12 Enter PIN.
13 Press cancel and re-enter correct PIN.
14 Enter amount of cash required.
15 Check make-up in rear view mirror.
16 Collect cash and receipt.
17 Further empty handbag to locate purse and place cash inside.
18 Place receipt in back of cheque book.
19 Re-check make-up again.
20 Drive forward 2 metres.
21 Reverse back to cash machine.
22 Retrieve card.
23 Re-empty hand bag, locate card holder and place card into the slot provided.
24 Restart stalled engine and pull away.
25 Drive for 2 to 3 miles.
26 Release handbrake.

Knobbly Knees Contests - The Sexual Exploitation of Men!

Just lately there has been a regrettable rise in the number of knobbly-knee contests held at local fêtes, galas and even vicarage garden parties.

This gross debasement of the male body, using the knees for amusement and titillation of the prurient or perverted, treats men as mere objects for others' pleasure.

Defenders of these sad displays say the men who enter knobbly-knees contests do so for their own reasons. This pathetic argument fails to note the social pressures imposed on reluctant men to expose themselves in this way.

Driven by the "dare" culture and fear of appearing wimpish, men are coerced into enduring the humiliation of knee nakedness.

In the worst cases they do it for drugs - the promise of a pint of Abbot sucks them into a downward spiral in which they become playthings for a gawping public.

This cattle market should be spurned by all politically correct persons.

(By kind permission of Christopher South, columnist for the Cambridge Evening News)

Man Speak

"It would take too long to explain"...*really means*..."I haven't got a clue how it works!"

"My wife doesn't understand me"...*really means*..."She's heard all my stories and is tired of them!"

"I can't find it"...*really means*..."I haven't actually looked but it didn't fall into my outstretched hands!"

"It's a man thing"...*really means*..."There is no rational thought pattern to it and it's not logical!"

"What did I do this time?"...*really means*..."What did you catch me out at this time?"

"I'm going to go for a quick drink on the way home"...*really means*..."See you at midnight!"

"That looks great"...*really means*..."Please don't try on any more dresses - I'm so bored!"

"Mmmm...That's interesting dear/love"...*really means*..."Are you actually still talking?"

Woman Speak

"Fine"...*really means*..."This is anything but fine and you need to be quiet now!"

"Nothing"...*really means*..."Oh, this is so something!"

"We need to talk"...*really means*..."I need to complain about something and you need to listen!"

"Go ahead"...*really means*..."I dare you to do that - if you do, you will really regret it!"

"That's OK"...*really means*..."You think that I'm happy - you could not be more wrong!"

"Thanks a lot"...*really means*..."You have just insulted/upset me and you are going to pay for this!"

"We need"...*really means*..."I want!"

"Loud sigh"...*really means*..."There are many words I could use but none would convey my disgust!"

Britain's Politically Correct Calendar

January

New Year

Some schools in the UK now use the terms "BCE" (Before Common Era) and "CE" (Common Era) instead of the well known terms "BC" and "AD". One explanation given for the reasoning behind this change was that "Many scholars and editors working today in the multicultural discipline of world history use terminology that does not impose the standards of one culture on others".

February

Valentine's Day

Lawyers warned that Valentine's Day could become an "expensive minefield" in the office. They said, "Sending a Valentine's Day card could constitute an unwanted sexual advance and lead to sexual harassment claims". They also said, "Someone who has received no cards might be sensitive and someone who receives 10 could find themselves accused of promiscuity."

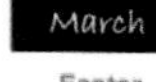

March

Easter

NHS officials in Grampian said staff could no longer celebrate Easter or take their traditional Easter break to avoid offending other religions. Health chiefs claimed that recognising the festival would insult Muslims and foreign staff saying, "The Easter holidays issue is a sensitive one but we are a multicultural organisation." No other Health Authorities in Scotland followed suit.

January

New Year

Some schools in the UK now use the terms "BCE" (Before Common Era) and "CE" (Common Era) instead of the well known terms "BC" and "AD". One explanation given for the reasoning behind this change was that "Many scholars and editors working today in the multicultural discipline of world history use terminology that does not impose the standards of one culture on others".

February

Valentine's Day

Lawyers warned that Valentine's Day could become an "expensive minefield" in the office. They said, "Sending a Valentine's Day card could constitute an unwanted sexual advance and lead to sexual harassment claims". They also said, "Someone who has received no cards might be sensitive and someone who receives 10 could find themselves accused of promiscuity."

March

Easter

NHS officials in Grampian said staff could no longer celebrate Easter or take their traditional Easter break to avoid offending other religions. Health chiefs claimed that recognising the festival would insult Muslims and foreign staff saying, "The Easter holidays issue is a sensitive one but we are a multicultural organisation." Thankfully no other Health Authorities in Scotland followed suit.

April

St George's Day

The company in charge of Salford City Council's housing stock told its maintenance workers that they must not fly any unauthorised accessories, including the flag of St George. An employee of the company said "Salford is increasingly becoming a multicultural city and the council has to be sensitive to how residents of other nationalities would react to England flags being displayed."

May

VE Day

A boy who wore a "VE Day Thanks" badge to school which depicted a little Union Jack was told that his badge was racist. He was forced to remove the badge he had been given by his grandfather to commemorate VE Day, despite the fact that people up and down the country were celebrating the anniversary of this important victory in Britain's battle for freedom.

June

Father's Day

The counselling service, Relate, said that pupils should be encouraged to make 'special person' cards instead of traditional Mother and Father's Day cards. Relate said that children living with single parents, step-parents or even parents of the same sex could be offended. They went on to say, "There are also ethnic and cultural influences to consider."

July

Sports Day

Children at a school in Scotland were told that they were not allowed to cheer and voice their support for their school house team on sports day. Romsey MP, Sandra Gidley, also said that sports days publicly humiliated children who finished last. She called the traditional annual competition her "pet hate" and accused schools of failing to consider the feelings of children with little sporting ability.

August

Summer Holidays

Officials in Blackpool were deployed to ensure that donkeys working on the beach in the summer season had a full hour off for 'lunch'. At the same time as the EU's Working Time Directive came into force, limiting British employees to a 48 hour week, the number of hours the donkeys were allowed to work was also fixed at 48 per week.

September

Ramadan

Two Scottish NHS Boards advised staff they should not eat at their desks during Ramadan and all vending machines should be removed from areas where Muslims worked, in case fasting Muslims were upset or offended. One said, "As a responsible and pro-active employer we will continue to promote a positive culture, which recognises and respects diversity both in our workforce and in the people we serve."

October

Trafalgar Day

During an event to mark the bi-centenary of the Battle of Trafalgar, the actor who was dressed as Nelson had to wear a lifejacket over his costume whilst he was being transported in an RNLI lifeboat to the event, which was taking place on the Thames.

November

Remembrance Day

A man who worked in a Secondary School which had 'special needs' status purchased a dozen Remembrance Poppies and took them to school intending to have brief, informal chats about their meaning with the children. He only had the opportunity to do this twice before hearing a colleague telling his boss that he had been "indoctrinating the kids".

December

Christmas

A school had a "Festive Period" concert and one of the songs the children sang was "Little Donkey". However, the lyrics were changed from "Little donkey, carry Mary" to "Little donkey, carry Lucy" as the name Mary was thought to be too religious and teachers were worried that it could cause offence.

Silly Signs

Sign on a supermarket pineapple:
"Suitable for vegetarians"

PLEASE NOTE
These signs aren't meant to be funny but they either have an unintended double meaning, use an "interesting" choice of language or are a statement of the bloomin' obvious….!
Fasting and Prayer Conference:
"Includes meals"
Hospital Maternity Ward:
"No children allowed"
Office Sign:
"Toilet out of order. Please use floor below"
Advert for Shower Gel:
"So citrusy you won't know whether to wash with it or drink it. Not suitable for consumption"
Frozen Dinner:
"Serving Suggestion—Defrost"

PUSH
Automatic Door:
"Push to operate"
UPSTAIRS
Department Store:
"Bargain basement upstairs"
Washing Machine at Launderette:
"Please remove all your clothes when the light goes out"
Farm Gate:
"Cattle please close the gate"
TV Remote Control:
"Not dishwasher safe"
Chocolate Novelty CD:
"Do not place this product into any electrical equipment"

Tattoo Parlour:
"Tattoos done while you wait"
Foaming Face Wash:
"May contain foam"
Can of Pepper Spray:
"May irritate eyes"
Kettle: "The appliance is switched on by setting the on/off switch to the 'on' position"
ON-OFF
Pay and Display Sign:
"Pay (at machine)
& Display (on windscreen)"
Toothpaste Tube:
"Directions: Apply to your toothbrush, brush your teeth thoroughly and rinse"

Packet of Toffees:
"Factory—no nuts on site"
Rain Gauge
"Suitable for outdoor use"
Seeds
ZOO
Sign at Zoo:
"Please do not feed the animals. If you have any suitable food, please give it to the guard"
Shower Cap:
"Fits one head"
Baking Potatoes:
"Ideal for baking"
500 Piece Puzzle:
"Some assembly required"

The Real Rules Of Life

Kids Rules

Kids Rules

Our education system has given some children an unrealistic expectation of life. Here are some rules which might help them to cope better in the *real* world.

Rule 1

Life is not fair—get used to it.

Rule 2

If you think your teacher is tough, wait until you get a boss.

Rule 3

Be nice to "Nerds". Chances are you may end up working for one.

Rule 4

Your teacher may not correct your spelling but be assured that if your CV is full of spelling mistakes you are very unlikely to be hired.

Rule 5

If you mess up, it's neither your parents' fault nor anyone else's for that matter. Don't blame someone else for your mistakes—learn from them.

Rule 6

Starting off by stacking shelves is not beneath your dignity. Your grandparents had a different word for this - they called it an "opportunity".

Rule 7

You will not get a huge salary just after you have left school. You won't be in charge of a company, with a flash car and perks until you earn the position.

Rule 8

Your school may have scrapped winners and losers, abolished fail marks and toyed with the idea of introducing the concept of "deferred success". Please note that this does not bear the slightest resemblance to real life.

Rule 9

Even though it is possible for completely talentless people to become famous with apparently very little effort - it is not the norm. It is easier to chase your dreams whilst your feet are on the ground and your head is out of the clouds.

Rule 10

If you think life is boring now, wait until you are responsible for your own home and have to wash up, clean, dust, put the bins out, mow the lawn and read the same story over and over and over again to your child!

The End

Christmas Political Correctness

Christmas Crackers

A survey of Christmas cards showed that fewer than one per cent of Christmas cards had anything to do with Jesus. Most businesses used the phrase "Season's Greetings" instead of referring to Christmas. Many had even completely wiped out any reference to Christmas from their cards by removing all the traditional favourites such as angels, the Three Kings and even Santa Claus.

After the Pretoria Pit disaster of 21 December 1910, which killed nearly 350 men from Westhoughton and the surrounding areas, Christmas 1910 became known as "Black Christmas". Relatives of survivors were having a commemoration in a nursing home and displayed posters of remembrance only to be ordered to take them down as they contained the word 'Black' which could be offensive to black people.

A man who walked into a bank in Scotland and congratulated them on displaying a Christmas tree was surprised to be told by the Manager that, although they had managed to erect the Christmas tree, they had not hung any lights around it in case they electrocuted a customer.

The management at a Marks & Spencer store in the South East of England stopped playing "I'm dreaming of a White Christmas" over the store's music system after a complaint from a shopper who said the song was racist.

The annual Christmas lights switch-on in Scarborough had to be cancelled after organisers said that they could not meet the costs of all the health and safety regulations needed to enable the event to go ahead.

The Government conciliation body, ACAS, said that employers could put themselves at risk of an age discrimination claim if the music or entertainment at office parties was obviously aimed at younger staff. They also said that holding a Christmas raffle with alcohol as prizes could offend Muslims.

Christmas Crackers

A woman received a note from the local nursery saying that her child was to play a "snowperson" in what can only be described as an "interesting" version of a nativity play.

A Vicar asked his choir to sing "God Rest Ye Merry People" instead of "God Rest Ye Merry Gentlemen" at Christmas time so as not to offend women.

Sure Start Playgroups up and down the country deliberately avoided celebrating Christmas. A playgroup in Sheffield said, "We will not be referring to Christmas because we are not affiliated to any one religion" and a toddlers' group in London intentionally avoided reference to Christmas in their December events. A nursery in Brent said, "We are having a winter children's party. It encompasses all religions." A further centre in Hackney said, "We're not having Christmas parties; our groups are just having parties. We've got quite a few people of different faiths, so we can't just have the one Christmas party when there's all the other faiths."

A warning sign on a set of Christmas tree lights said, "For indoor or outdoor use only".

Knowland Grove School in Norwich replaced the traditional Christmas nativity play with a "Festival of Light" where the two youngest age-groups presented pieces on Christmas and Christingles. The children in Year Two performed a poem about Hanukkah and the children in Year Three explained Diwali. The Headteacher said, "We decided this year to take a slightly different approach with our end of term production to include a look at some of the other great cultural festivals of the world."

Since the early 20th century pantomime characters have thrown sweets to children in the audience as a Christmas treat. However, those running a pantomime in Lancashire decided to ban this 'risky business' from the show as they were concerned they could be sued if anyone was injured by a flying sweet.

Christmas Crackers

Oakwood College in Rotherham took traditional Christmas turkey off the school menu and replaced it with Muslim halal chicken. After an outcry from parents, the college said that they would offer a choice of either traditional turkey or halal chicken to pupils.

Operation Christmas Child (run by the charity Samaritan's Purse), which sends packages from donors to deprived youngsters in countries ravaged by war and famine, asked donors not to pack the shoeboxes with anything to do with Christmas. Britons filled 1.13million shoeboxes in 1 year alone but were told not to include stories from the Bible, images of Jesus or any other Christian literature with their package in case Muslims were offended. The charity said "Anything we find in the boxes which has a religious nature will be removed."

Pupils at a primary school were told by a teacher that Santa was not real and only 'small children' believed in Father Christmas'. The teacher used material which went on to explain that thousands of letters sent by children to Santa every year were actually answered by the Post Office. Parents criticised teachers for taking the 'magic' out of Christmas and said that the festivities had been 'ruined' for their children.

Organisers of a village Christmas party were told they must carry out a risk assessment on their mince pies. Local council officials also said that posters would have to be displayed at the party in Embsay, in the Yorkshire Dales, warning villagers that the pies contained nuts and suet pastry. The cocoa content and temperature of the hot chocolate also had to be checked.

A school carol concert in Dudley was scrapped after a local resident objected to the application for an entertainment licence needed to enable the concert to go ahead.

A council in London banned staff from putting up Christmas lights and decorations in case they hurt themselves in the process.

Warning: Christmas is cancelled!

The Politically Correct Olympics

... how long before this becomes a reality?

It was decided that the London Olympics would be a fantastic opportunity to showcase Britain's commitment to Political Correctness and Health and Safety.

With the eyes of the world due to be on London for the Olympics, the British Government felt it had a duty to show other poorer "less enlightened" countries the error of their ways and encourage them to follow Britain's lead.

The first decision the Government made was to ask their public relations consultants to change the Olympic logo from the previously chosen design to "PCUK" so that merchandise the world over would be branded with a reference to Political Correctness.

Then the Government turned its attention to the selection of British athletes. In order to ensure that the athletes "represented the community", it was decided that there would be a quota system for entrants along the lines of race. As white athletes were known to be seriously under-represented in various fields, many black athletes had to be de-selected and less qualified white athletes were given their places to ensure that the make up of the team "reflected the country".

In the face of tears from the black athletes whose years of hard work had led them to the dream of a lifetime, only for it to be so unfairly snatched away, the Government said that "Equality" issues had to be at the heart of the Olympics. They said without "Diversity, Diversity, Diversity" their commitment to Political Correctness would be shallow.

The Government announced that the opening ceremony would be used to show off the cultural diversity of London. No single group would be excluded because of their age, sex, race, colour, disability, sexuality, language, religion, shoe size, table manners, eyesight, burger preference, height, computer skills or nut allergies. There was even to be a spot for "Ginger Hair Twirling" and "Fat and Proud Belly Dancing". The organisers boasted that this display would take three days instead of the usual few hours so as to fit everything in.

It was declared that all road signs in the surrounding areas were to be changed to show road distances in kilometres as it was considered "easier for visiting foreigners to understand".

The signage at the Olympics was to be in the 300 languages thought to be spoken in London. Binoculars would be issued to the athletes so that they could read the 200 feet (61 metre) signs as they passed them. To ensure there was no perceived bias towards the home nation, English was to be at the top of the sign so that it would be the least readable language of them all - despite being the most widely used across the world.

All commentaries would also be made in 300 languages. Experts said that this would mean the games would last for 6 weeks instead of the usual 16 days but this was said to be non-negotiable. The athletes were told that the Games were not, after all, about their talents. They were about the Government's commitment to Political Correctness and "inclusivity" was the name of the game.

In the name of "Equality", the Government decided there should be no "sexist" barriers preventing women from competing against men.

The unification of the male and female competitions was proclaimed to be a huge victory against the alleged historic sex discrimination that had been perpetrated against women.

Despite massive protests from women who wanted to keep their own events, the Government insisted that men and women were now truly equal and patted themselves on the back for achieving this admirable feat.

Many "reasonable adjustments" were also made to the Olympic venue, the track and various items of sporting equipment in order to comply with Disability Discrimination Legislation.

Even the hurdles were fitted with ramps!

After an extensive risk assessment it was decided that the javelins were "too sharp to be safe" and were ordered to be made more rounded. Boxing was to be banned as it was far too violent and replaced with a hugging contest. The 'shot put' was ruled out as Health and Safety inspectors said that the angle at which the 'shot' was thrown was likely to cause neck strain and it could be dropped on a competitor's toe. The hammer throw was excluded as this could encourage violence amongst viewers. The triple jump was abandoned as not everyone could be expected to hop, skip and jump. Lastly, both the pole vault and the high jump were ditched as it was evident that contestants would be contravening "The Work At Height Regulations".

The Government stated that there should be no winners or losers at the Olympics as this could have a negative effect on those taking part and also traumatise those watching.

Those who were any good would be given a handicap so that those who were useless would have a head start.

Contestants in track events were told they all had to cross the line at the same time so that there could be an immediate group hug after they had finished.

Gold medals were to be awarded to everyone who took part after the Government wholeheartedly endorsed the mentality of many schools in Britain which decreed that "everyone must have prizes". As a result, the podiums were very long and very wide so that they could contain all the participants of each event - all "winners".

National anthems were abandoned as it was feared they would encourage unpleasant nationalism and "I'd like to give the world a hug" was adopted as the official song of the Olympics.

Finally, it was decided that the lighting of the Olympic Torch would not be completed. In addition to the law against lighting up in public places, it was thought, from a Health and Safety point of view, it would be far too dangerous to have a naked flame.

And so it was decreed that the icing on the cake of these Politically Correct Games was that the traditional Olympic Torch would have to be extinguished!

Illustrations by Beverley Rodgers (www.BeverleyRodgers.com)

January

New Year

Some schools in the UK now use the terms "BCE" (Before Common Era) and "CE" (Common Era) instead of the well known terms "BC" and "AD". One explanation given for the reasoning behind this change was that "Many scholars and editors working today in the multicultural discipline of world history use terminology that does not impose the standards of one culture on others".

February

Valentine's Day

Lawyers warned that Valentine's Day could become an "expensive minefield" in the office. They said, "Sending a Valentine's Day card could constitute an unwanted sexual advance and lead to sexual harassment claims". They also said, "Someone who has received no cards might be sensitive and someone who receives 10 could find themselves accused of promiscuity."

March

Easter

NHS officials in Grampian said staff could no longer celebrate Easter or take their traditional Easter break to avoid offending other religions. Health chiefs claimed that recognising the festival would insult Muslims and foreign staff saying, "The Easter holidays issue is a sensitive one but we are a multicultural organisation." No other Health Authorities in Scotland followed suit.

What Can Be Done?

If this book has made you want to do something to stop the advance of Political Correctness (PC), there is plenty that can be done!

Some of those who support PC often have good intentions but they need to realise that they are actually doing so much damage. **You can really achieve a great deal by personally challenging PC** whenever you see or hear it. However, if you are not in a position to do this, why not contact the Campaign Against Political Correctness and let them do it for you?

For further ideas about helping to put an end to PC, to see many more stories and examples of PC, to sign a petition against PC or to buy merchandise to show your opposition to PC you can get in touch with the Campaign Against Political Correctness on any of the contact points below.

Website:
www.CAPC.co.uk

Address:
Campaign Against Political Correctness
Trevose House, Orsett Street,
London SE11 5PN

e-mail:
info@capc.co.uk

If you would like to join the Campaign Against Political Correctness or make a donation now please just send your details to the address above. There is no minimum membership fee. At the time of writing, new members donating £20 or over (£30 or over for a couple) will each receive a complimentary lapel badge. *Please make any cheques payable to 'CAPC'.*

Many thanks!

And finally ...

... Whenever you see or hear the phrase "Political Correctness" give a thought to the very appropriate anagram that comes from these words – "Lies Control Practices"!

Buy Both Politically Correct Scrapbooks Now!

The Original Politically Correct Scrapbook
(ISBN 978-0-9552078-0-8)

£7.99 for 1 copy
OR
£22 for 3 copies

Free P&P in UK

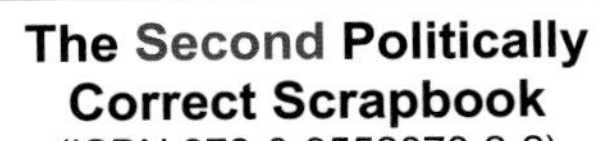

The Second Politically Correct Scrapbook
(ISBN 978-0-9552078-2-2)

£8.99 for 1 copy
OR
£25 for 3 copies

Free P&P in UK

A Duo of Both Politically Correct Scrapbooks

£15 for 2 copies

1 copy of The **Original** PC Scrapbook and 1 copy of The **Second** PC Scrapbook

Free P&P in UK

A Trio of Both Politically Correct Scrapbooks

£23 for your choice of 3 copies

Simply choose your combination of 2 copies of 1 book and 1 copy of the other book

Free P&P in UK

ORDER ONLINE
with a credit card via the book icon on:

www.CAPC.co.uk

ORDER BY POST:

Please make your cheque or postal order payable to "CAPC" and send it with the following form (or a copy) to the address below.

Please send me:

- ______ **copy/copies of The Original PC Scrapbook(s) (£7.99 for 1, £22 for 3)**
- ______ **copy/copies of The Second PC Scrapbook(s) (£8.99 for 1, £25 for 3)**
- ______ **Duo(s) of PC Scrapbooks** (1 copy of each book) **(£15)**
- ______ **Trio(s) of PC Scrapbooks -** your combination choice: ____ 'Original' PC Scrapbook(s) ____ 'Second' PC Scrapbook(s)
  (2 copies of 1 book & 1 copy of the other book) (**£23**)

I am enclosing a cheque/P.O. (payable to "CAPC") for £_______ (all prices include FREE Postage & Packing in the UK)

Name: ____

Address: ____

____

____________________________ **Postcode:** ______________

Contact number: ______________ **e-mail address:** ______________

Book Offer, C/o CAPC, Trevose House, Orsett Street, London SE11 5PN

We will make every effort to post books as quickly as possible upon receipt of your order. If you have a special deadline please let us know when ordering and we will endeavour to meet it. Our present contact number (and fax number) is 07092 040916.